READY TO SELL YOUR BUSINESS?

ADRIAN SPITTERS FCSI, CFP, FMA
SENIOR WEALTH ADVISOR

Heart Beat
PRODUCTIONS

READY TO SELL YOUR BUSINESS?

or

Transfer it to the Next Generation

Assante
WEALTH MANAGEMENT

Be well-advised.

Copyright 2017 by Adrian Spitters, FCSI, CFP, FMA

ISBN: 978-1-895112-39-9

Published by
HeartBeat Productions Inc.
Box 633 Abbotsford, BC Canada V2T 6Z8
email: heartbeatproductions@gmail.com
604.852.3761

Edited by Dr. Win Wachsmann
Cover design, artwork: Dr. Carrie Wachsmann
Cover Photo: dacosta / 123RF Stock Photo

All rights reserved. No portion of this book may be reproduced in any form without the written permission of the publisher.

Printed in USA

HeartBeat PRODUCTIONS

THIS BOOK IS DEDICATED
TO BUSINESS OWNERS
WHO DON'T
WANT TO WORK FOREVER

TABLE OF CONTENTS

Chapter 1 Introduction 9

Chapter 2 Challenges 15

Chapter 3 Need for a plan 21

Chapter 4 Step 1 - Visualize Your Future 25

Chapter 5 Step 2 - Analyze Your Reality 27

Chapter 6 Step 3 - Commit to Creating a Plan 31

Chapter 7 Step 4 - Create a Solid Wealth Foundation 33

Chapter 8 Step 5 - Design Your Business Transition Plan . 37

Chapter 9 Step 6 - Execute Your Plan 39

Chapter 10 Step 7 - Achieve Your Desired Future 41

Chapter 11 Step 8 - Share Your Family's Wealth 43

Chapter 12 How do I know? 47

Chapter 13 The Role of Advisors 49

Chapter 14 Selling Your Business 57

Chapter 15 Tax Strategies 59

Chapter 16 Enough 67

Chapter 17 Preparing Your Family 73

Chapter 18 How can I Help You? 75

Chapter 19 How do you start? 83

Chapter 20 Adrian Spitters & Assante 87

Chapter 21 Business Wealth Planning Checklist 93

Chapter 22 What Type of Advisor Should I Choose? 109

Chapter 23 What Can I Expect in Terms of Fees? 113

Chapter 24 What Services Should be Offered? 119

Chapter 25 50 Ways Wealth Advisors Benefit Their Clients 123

Chapter 26 Conclusion 129

Chapter 27 Your Optimal Portfolio Solution™ 133

Chapter 28 The Second Opinion Portfolio Audit™ 149

Chapter 29 Appendix ....
Tax Planning for the Sale of Your Business 157

To business owners who don't want to work forever

One day your business will change hands...

Will you transfer your business to your children, extended family, or sell to a third party?

Will it be on your terms?

CHAPTER 1
INTRODUCTION

Most business owners don't have time to think too far ahead into the future. That's because they're busy attending to the needs of today: producing high-quality products, overseeing employees, and managing the mind-boggling number of details that go into owning a business.

If they *do* think about the future, it's usually about new government regulations, how the recent elections will impact their business and perhaps new market opportunities for their products.

The truly long-term decisions, like when to sell or transition your business (not to mention how to do it), are mentally filed away under the heading, "Bridges to cross when I've come to it."

But that bridge may be a lot closer than you think.

No time to deal with the issue

Understandably, most business owners have great difficulty in setting aside the time to plan for the future of their business in addition to working on their business.

To quote John F. Kennedy, *"The time to mend the roof is when the sun is shining."*

It is the planning for the future of your business while the sun is shining that will help protect your business, and ultimately your family, from the rainstorms that loom ahead.

You see, recently conducted surveys[1] of privately-owned family businesses, including businesses across North America, report that approximately 40% of business owners expect to exit their family business in the next five years. That number goes up to a whopping 70% within the next ten years.

---

[1] *The information from these surveys was derived from various sources, including Deloitte, PWC, Laird, Tyne, CFIB and MassMutual.*

These statistics are a direct result of the fact that baby-boomers are nearing retirement.

A significant number of these business owners indicate that they will be relying on the ongoing success of their business to finance their future lifestyle – either by selling the business, or from collecting a salary or dividend after they exit day-to-day management.

All this applies to business owners like you.

So, ask yourself:

1. Do you have a plan in place to increase the value of your business before it's time to sell?
2. Do you have a plan in place that will enable you to transfer your business to your family or sell to a third party?
3. Have you planned how to retire on your terms, instead of being forced to transfer or sell your business on someone else's?
4. Are you proactively preparing a successor who will enable the continuity of your business?

Or are you one of the 65% of business owners who haven't planned that far ahead?[2]

---

[2] http://www.bdo.ca/en/Services/Advisory/Business-Transition/pages/The-BDO-SuccessCare-Program.aspx

It's true: most business owners haven't planned for the day when they will transition or sell their business. That makes them vulnerable to an **involuntary sale**, meaning they will be forced to sell their business due to death, disability, or other reasons.

As you can see, the question of when and how to transition your business is something that needs to be answered sooner rather than later.

The first step is to have a plan. Having a plan in place *now* can save you untold time and trouble in the future…and it can also help ensure that when the time *does* come to transition your business, you do it *right*.

The stakes are high. For an overwhelming number of business owners, the sale of their business will be their primary source of income for retirement.

That's why it's crucial that they get it right. Otherwise, they will deny themselves the chance at much-needed income during a time when every dollar counts.

For others, their major goal is to keep their business in the family. But transitioning your business, even to your own children, is a long and complex process.

Finally, *everyone* wants to cement their legacy and good name long after the transaction takes place.

I know that as **business owners**... your business is one of the most important in the entire world. I understand that owning a business isn't easy. Yet I also know that the decision to one-day sell or transfer out of your business can be just as difficult.

My name is Adrian Spitters. I'm a Senior Wealth Advisor with Assante Capital Management Ltd. As the child of a farmer, I can appreciate the hard work you've put into establishing a successful business.

I've prepared this special book just for you. In just a few short pages, we'll look at some of the challenges facing business owners who want to quit working someday, what the most successful business owners are doing now, and where you can get additional help.

One of my goals is to give you ideas on how to plan for *your* eventual transition into retirement and have peace of mind.

CHAPTER 2

THE CHALLENGES FACING BUSINESS OWNERS WHO WANT TO QUIT WORK SOMEDAY

Here are two plain and simple truths.

The **first** is that no matter how much you enjoy what you do, you probably don't want to do it forever.

At some point in our lives, we all want to wind down, explore other interests, and just generally live life at a slower pace. It's called retirement.

The **second** truth is that retirement is becoming increasingly difficult and expensive. This is especially true for business owners like you.

There are unique challenges you face that must be overcome in order for you to sell or transition your business and retire the way you've always dreamed.

Some Challenges You Will Face:

1. How to determine the value of your business
2. Where and how to find the right buyer
3. How to choose the right time to sell
4. Deciding whether to transition your business to a family member or sell to a non-related party
5. Ensuring you have sufficient assets to secure you and your family's future
6. Determining whether selling your business will bring in enough proceeds to fund your retirement and other financial goals
7. Ensuring the orderly payment and transition of ownership/management of your business to your successor/heir
8. How to minimize the taxes that come from selling your business

And the biggest Challenge?

You don't want to think about leaving

Underlying many of the reasons for failing to address the inevitable transition of their business is the fear entrepreneurs have of leaving what they have worked so hard to build. The business is their life and they do not want to give up control.

We can show you how you can gradually delegate control while finding a way to still employ your unique abilities. You can develop a track that will allow you to slowly step away from the business while doing what is needed to protect your family and the business.

And what about Conflicts with Family/ Employees?

It's amazing how often family dynamics become almost insurmountable when thinking about transitioning your business.

One or more of your children may be working in your business while others have never joined or left the business to explore other interests. In family gatherings, the discussion will rarely move in that direction.

However, everyone is giving it some thought. And that applies to your children and their spouses as well. You love them all dearly but they will have different expectations of what the transition should look like.

As a result, many business owners are reluctant to attempt reconciling the differing personalities, values and expectations that exist in their family unit.

Who wants to start a family argument over the Thanksgiving or Christmas turkey?

By now you know your hot buttons and those of your family members. So, the easiest thing is to bite your lip or walk out of the room if that can be done circumspectly.

So, you may try to defer the decisions and discussions, but there comes a time when all these issues will need to be addressed.

With the appropriate structures in place, you can address any potential conflict in advance and prepare the way to move ahead with a transition plan.

But it's Still A few Years Off

Now you may be thinking, "Retirement is still a few years off. Why do I have to think about this now?"

The answer is that by thinking and planning *now*, you can drastically improve your chances of retiring how you want to in the future. That's because, when it comes to selling your business, you can either do it **by choice** or **by necessity**.

To sell by necessity means that you really have no other option than to sell your business, often as quickly as possible, to the highest bidder (who may be looking at the stresses you face and as a result will not be offering fair market value at all). Poor health, bankruptcy, or even a dramatic change in the industry may force your hand to sell.

The main problem with selling by necessity is that you often have to settle for a lower price. A secondary problem is that once your business is sold, you will suddenly find yourself without a livelihood, and with no idea whether you have enough money on which to retire.

Selling by choice, on the other hand, means that *you* choose the timing and terms of your sale. *You* get to decide who you sell to and for how much.

Best of all, you can coordinate your sale within an overall retirement plan, factoring in your investments, taxes, and other financial goals.

The result? The knowledge that you can retire, stay retired, and make retirement everything you want it to be.

CHAPTER 3

THE NEED FOR A PLAN

There's one thing that separates a business owner who sells voluntarily from those who sell by necessity: the former has a transition plan.

No matter how young or old you are, you need to have a plan. Saying "It's too early" is like saying, "I don't need to put my seatbelt on yet, I just pulled out of the garage. I'll wait until I'm on the highway."

The fact is, it's *never* too early. The sooner you have a plan, the sooner you can more ably avoid the unexpected bumps that every business owner faces at some point or another.

General Dwight Eisenhower, former president of the United States, said it this way:

"Failing to plan is planning to fail."

The Basics of a Good Transition Plan

Remember that a *plan* is a series of steps, determined in advance, designed to help you reach a specific objective.

The word "objective" is especially important. After all, you can't know what steps to take until you first know where you want to go.

What might a transition/succession plan include?

The formal succession plan includes information about matters such as:

1. The identity of the successor or successors;
2. How the successor will be trained for his or her role;
3. The roles of other key managers during the transition;
4. The mechanics for the purchase or sale of shares in the business;
5. The distribution of ownership;
6. Taxation and legal considerations;
7. Financial considerations;
8. Retirement considerations;

9. A procedure for monitoring the process and dealing with disputes and problems; and
10. A timetable.

So, what might a transition plan look like?

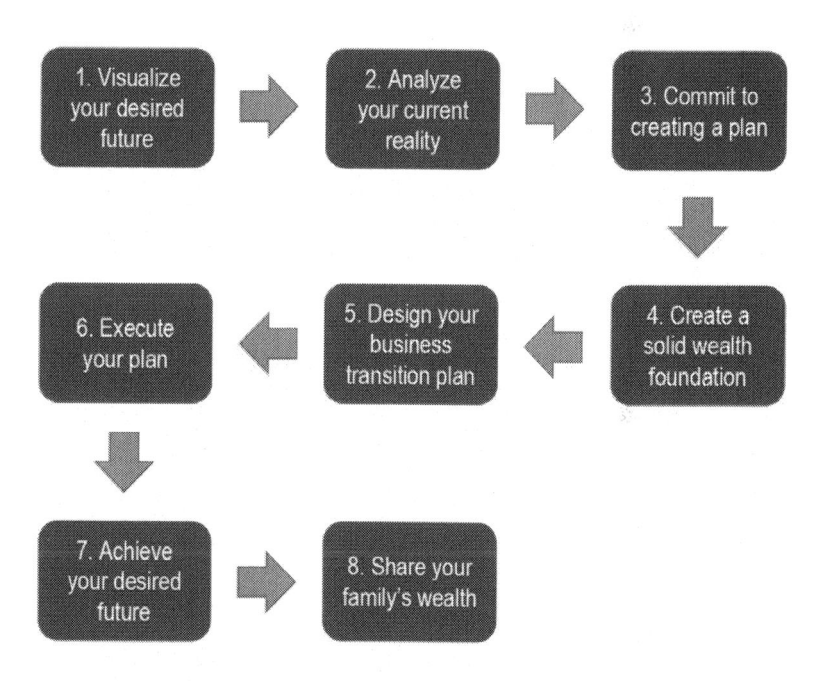

1. Visualize your desired future → 2. Analyze your current reality → 3. Commit to creating a plan ↓ 4. Create a solid wealth foundation ← 5. Design your business transition plan ← 6. Execute your plan ↓ 7. Achieve your desired future → 8. Share your family's wealth

I would like to suggest the following guideline for a business transition plan. In the following chapters, we will look at each one of these eight components.

Please understand that this will not be an exhaustive discussion. For detailed steps and a wide range of planning documents, please contact the author. As a skilled advisor, I have a extensive resources available to assist you to make the best decisions possible.

This book is an introduction to the business transition process - a task that may take several months and many conversations with family members and advisors.

CHAPTER 4

STEP 1:
VISUALIZE YOUR DESIRED FUTURE

1. Visualize your desired future

The first thing your transition plan should contain, then, is a **vision** of your desired future. A **vision** is a vivid picture of your future based on your goals, dreams and desires. Having a vision helps to clarify what is a priority for your life.

Remember, it's hard to get lost if you know where you are going.

Here is a sampling of the many questions that can be addressed. Feel free to add to the list.
1. What are your core values and principles?
2. Why do you continue to operate your business?

3. What do you want to accomplish in your life?
4. What dreams do you have for yourself and your family?
5. What legacy would you like to leave?
6. Will you stay on in your business and continue in some fashion?
7. When (if ever) will you be ready for a change in lifestyle?
8. Have you discussed the above questions with your spouse?
9. Does your vision of retirement match up with your spouse's?
10. Have you discussed passing your business to your child(ren) working in the business while balancing non-business child(ren)'s interests?

I'm sure you can think of more questions to ponder.

Sometimes it is helpful to meet with a Wealth Advisor who will take the time to get to know your true fears, challenges, advantages, excitements, opportunities, lifetime goals and aspirations for you, your family, business, and legacy.

Telling a stranger about your aspirations isn't easy. However, if you think of your advisor as a valued confidant who will help you plan and achieve your vision, the process becomes less scary.

Their role is to help you visualize what your future could hold, and then create a summary report outlining the steps you should take to achieve it.

You will find a sample **Business Wealth Planning Checklist** – Chapter 21

CHAPTER 5

STEP 2: ANALYZE YOUR CURRENT REALITY

2. Analyze your current reality

An effective transition plan should include a thorough analysis of what I like to call your **current reality**.

This step involves exploring all areas of your personal, family and business life that can have a financial impact on your wealth.

Think of it as an inventory of what you have to work with.

1. What is your current income?
2. What kind of expenses do you have?

3. What assets do you have? Real estate, stocks and bonds, RRSP's? Are you minimizing personal taxes on these non-business assets?
4. What kind of liabilities do you have? Short term, long term?
5. How is your current health? What does your future hold?
6. Are you maximizing income splitting opportunities with family members?
7. Are you running your business as a proprietor, partnership or corporation? Do you know how to minimize tax exposure on your business income in each scenario?
8. If you run your business as a proprietor, do you understand how incorporation can save taxes in the years leading to retirement?
9. Do you understand how a Business Partnership could create tax savings?
10. If you operate your business through a corporation here are some considerations:
    10.1 Does your corporate structure ensure that your shares can "roll" to children in the event of your death rather than being taxed?

10.2 Do you know if your shares will qualify for the lifetime Capital Gains Exemption?

10.3 Have you obtained advice about whether you need a separate holding corporation?

10.4 Will your corporate structure allow for the most tax-effective transfer of the operation to family members?

10.5 Do you understand how corporately held insurance can create a tax efficient succession plan?

As you can see, these are just a few of the questions that need to be addressed.

A discussion with a Family Wealth Advisor will bring many more questions to the forefront.

WARNING: What if you are separated, divorced or thinking about either?

The following is just an introduction and should not be construed as tax advice.

As a family wealth advisor, I have seen how marriage breakdown and separation/divorce can wreak havoc on relationships and with it impact the long-term health of business and business relationships.

Married life is supposed to be forever, but according to Canada government statistics, some 40% of marriages dissolve before they reach their 30th anniversary.[3]

Separation or divorce can have a significant impact on the health, stability and future of your business.

How you approach separation and the division of personal and business assets will have long-term tax implications for you, your spouse and your company.

Canadian tax rules for spouses are very clear and specific and differ from civil definitions.

Three tax areas which will impact your business are:

1. Spousal attribution rules,

2. Spousal transfer Rollover and

3. Capital gains Exemptions.

If you are separated, divorced or considering either, please contact your wealth advisor who will put you in touch with a competent tax professional.

As you can see this analysis process will require a lot of thought and planning.

You will find a sample **Business Wealth Planning Checklist** – Chapter 21

---

[3] https://www.bdo.ca/en-ca/insights/tax/tax-articles/tax-implications-of-separation-or-divorce-for-a-business-owner-manager/

CHAPTER 6

STEP 3: COMMIT TO CREATING A BUSINESS TRANSITION PLAN

3. Commit to creating a plan

After examining some of the questions in previous chapters, you can see how important it is to make a plan.

Your next step should be to commit to creating a plan.

This means setting time aside to compile a list of all the questions (and answers if you have them) about every aspect of your business and personal life.

It's not about having time, but about making time.

In the same way, you don't always have time to play with your grandchildren, you know you will make time to create memories and form bonds that will be remembered for many years to come.

Yes, the process may seem overwhelming.

However, just like every task you've ever taken on, it begins with that first step, that first shovelful, that first foundation.

How do you eat an elephant? One mouthful at a time. It may seem that this thinking and planning process is just like eating an elephant.

As you examine all the different parts of your business, you will soon realize that your lifetime of effort has created a living, breathing entity that will provide for you and your family for many years to come.

That accomplishment is something to be celebrated.

All those early, lonely hours, all that blood and sweat and all those tears have resulted in tangible and intangible assets of which you can be proud.

You have one more step, one more challenge ahead of you. To structure your business in such a way as to maximize the benefit for you and your family.

CHAPTER 7

STEP 4: CREATE A SOLID WEALTH FOUNDATION

4. Create a solid wealth foundation

This is all about you and your family's needs.

Your plan should also help determine what you *need* to reach your objective. For example:

1. Do you need to enhance the value of your business before you can sell it?
2. Does the future of your business include your children or extended family?

3. Do you need to minimize future taxes so that the sale or transition of your business will not complicate things?

4. Do you need a higher return on your investments or less risk so that your wealth will be more secure?

5. Do you need a will and estate plan to ensure your family will be taken care of should anything unexpected happen?

6. Do you need to simplify your business because you are spread too thin? Or do you need to expand and diversify to prevent all your eggs from staying in one basket?

These are just a few of the questions to ponder.

Like many business owners, your wealth is tied up in your business. Once you have sold your business, you need to create a solid investment foundation to manage the proceeds from the sale of your business.

You will want to examine your needs with respect to investing the proceeds from the sale of your business or the cash you put aside before transferring your business to your children to secure your retirement.

This will involve examining and quantifying your:
- risk tolerance
- liquidity requirements
- growth expectations
- insurance and annuity requirements
- income tax characteristics
- anticipated changes in lifestyle
- economic variables such as inflation and market volatility.

Because you have been busy running your business, you will probably not have spent much time examining long-term investment and wealth strategies.

What information you will have gleaned along the way will probably have come from accountants, lawyers and all those talking heads on TV who inhabit the financial channels and disseminate all that advice - some of which can be contradictory.

Where does one go for good, reliable advice?

Because we can't be experts in every field, we will need to speak with qualified, knowledgeable advisors.

Let me direct you to **Chapter 13 The Role of Advisors** where I will discuss in detail how to select a qualified and knowledgeable advisor.

CHAPTER 8

STEP 5:
DESIGN YOUR TRANSITION PLAN

5. Design your business transition plan

In the same way an architect helps you design and build a home or office building, you need to have a plan designed by wealth planning professionals.

This plan will protect and enhance the value of your business and minimize taxes in preparation for sale or transfer of your business.

Up until now, you will have been using your team of accountants and lawyers to structure and protect your business.

A business transition, however, can be a much more complex subject as you are learning from the previous chapters.

This requires a level of specialization that most lawyers and accountants don't have.

This is where a Wealth Advisor comes in.

A qualified, experienced and knowledgeable Wealth Advisor does not operate in a vacuum.

Over the years, the advisor will have built a team of wealth planning professionals on whom they can draw to help you design your plan.

The larger your business, the more complex the team will be.

They will work together with your lawyer and accountant(s) to analyze all possible solutions and design the best plan to preserve and enhance your wealth, and conceive a simple path for you to follow to achieve your desired future.

CHAPTER 9

STEP 6: EXECUTE YOUR PLAN

6. Execute your plan

Once you've developed *The Plan*, it will be time to implement *The Plan*.

This will involve meetings – lots of meetings between you and your advisors.

Meetings to discuss *The Plan* and then meetings to begin implementing *The Plan*.

Meetings to document any major changes in your personal or financial situation that require an adjustment to *The Plan*.

This may take months, and maybe even years if you start soon enough or have a number of years to go before you want to go out to pasture.

You must be aware that *The Plan* is not fixed in stone but is a living and flexible document that may require changes and improvements.

Every year, all levels of governments play around with the rules and regulations that affect our lives.

With every federal budget, tax relief is provided or tax regulations are increased.

Keeping up with all those changes requires knowledge (your advisors) and decisions on your part to modify your plan to maximize the benefit to you and your family.

The most important characteristic you will need is **patience**.

Patience with the process and patience with all the people in the process who will need to be involved and kept up to date.

During this time, hidden family stresses and issues may arise. Some family members may change their minds about the details while others may no longer want to be involved.

Also, see my comments about separation or divorce in Chapter 5.

CHAPTER 10

STEP 7: ACHIEVE YOUR DESIRED FUTURE

7. Achieve your desired future

Whew!

The implementation process is sometimes lengthy as the material is intense. It takes time to decide on the most efficient course of action for you to follow.

Once **The Plan** is complete, it will now be up to you to follow the steps in **Your Plan**.

Remember all those dreams we discussed in Chapter 4? By now you should see them coming to fruition.

Your long-suffering spouse is encouraging you to take a month or two and travel.

Isn't it time to let go and let the business get along without you?

It's very hard, but you deserve the time off. Who knows you may even like it.

And the grandkids? They want to see you more often.

Admit it. You want to see them as well - for a while.

CHAPTER 11

STEP 8: SHARE YOUR FAMILY'S WEALTH

8. Share your family's wealth

You've built your nest egg.

You've prepared for yourself and your family for the next generation(s).

You also want to help others.

With wise administration and strategic tax planning, you will be able to support your favourite charitable institution.

Whether it's the local food bank, a religious institution or funding high school and college scholarships and bursaries, your support will reap dividends for years to come.

Typically, giving can be achieved in four ways.

1. Giving your money directly.

You have found a cause, an organization or person who could use your financial assistance. You take out your check book or some cash and give it to them directly. Alternatively, you can give them securities that you own.

You may be offered a tax-deductible receipt if you give to an organization. If you give cash directly to a disadvantaged individual, you will not receive a tax deduction but you will receive their thanks and you will feel warm fuzzies because you have made a difference in someone's life.

In some cases, your giving will be anonymous, but in other times you will use your giving as a model and example for your family. Having compassion and being charitable is a valuable character trait.

*"We make a living by what we get, but
we make a life by what we give."*
Winston Churchill

2. You can give by volunteering your time.

Volunteering for a charity or a non-profit models responsible stewardship of time. Giving your time and energy to serve in a soup kitchen, for example, benefits the community. It also allows you to make a personal connection with the organization's workers and benefactors. In some cases, you receive immediate positive feedback from your involvement.

> *"Volunteering is at the very core of being a human. No one has made it through life without someone else's help."*
> **Heather French Henry**

3. Purchasing a life insurance policy

When you purchase a life insurance policy and name a charity as the sole beneficiary you generate a disproportionate benefit for that organization. The amount they receive will in all likelihood be much larger than you will ever be able to give them in cash or securities.

> *"The best way to find yourself is to lose yourself in the service of others."*
> **Mahatma Gandhi**

4. Establishing a charitable trust

Besides the immediate tax deductions, capital gains reductions and reduction of estate and income taxes upon your death, a charitable trust provides a longer benefit to the charity of your choice. A lump sum invested on behalf of a charity will pay longer dividends than just a single lump sum.

"We rise by lifting others."
Robert Ingersoll

CHAPTER 12

HOW DO I DO ALL THIS?

About Adrian Spitters
FCSI, CFP, FMA
Senior Wealth Advisor

I grew up on a dairy farm on Nicomen Island near Mission, BC and have immediate family and relatives operating dairy, poultry and crop farms.

As co-executor (with two brothers) of my father's estate, I know all too well the result of not having a proper farm transition plan in place.

Our dad had a poorly executed, unworkable Will and a non-existent farm succession plan.

This led to family discord. Despite receiving the majority of the assets, the brother who inherited the farm suffered financial distress and became insolvent. A proper transition plan would have helped him get the financial and farm management training he needed.

Today, I work as a Senior Wealth Advisor with Assante Capital Management Ltd., a leading Canadian wealth management firm with extensive experience in family business transitions. In my work with Assante, I provide wealth advisory services to family businesses. This includes helping them grow, protect and preserve their family assets, wealth and legacy.

In my 29 years in the business, I've seen: that all Canadians, especially business owners, need and want personalized financial advice that helps them achieve their life goals.

It is very clear to me that whether you have a transition plan in place or not, one day you will transfer your business to your children, extended family or sell to a third party. The question is, will it be on your terms **(voluntarily)**, or someone else's **(involuntarily)**?

To that end, I have acquired great expertise by working with the wealth planning specialists at the **Wealth Planning Group** of Assante Private Client, a division of CI Private Counsel LP.

I specialize in developing specific and personalized strategies for each of my business clients.

I work to enhance their knowledge, provide guidance, and create peace of mind for each of them to enjoy.

CHAPTER 13

THE ROLE OF ADVISORS

Getting the Help You Need: Building Your Transition Team

Throughout this book, I've written about talking with advisors and experts.

Successfully planning for and ultimately selling your business will almost certainly require some expert help. There are so many legal, accounting, tax, and insurance implications that it's all but impossible for you to do it all on your own.

Getting a qualified valuation of your business is also vital. **Fair market value** (for example) can be a very sticky issue with tax authorities, and trying to hand over your business to your immediate or extended family at a "good" price can have unintended (and serious) consequences.

Most business owners feel busy enough without having to contemplate the complex – and sometimes unpleasant – possibility of selling or transitioning their business someday. But unless they're planning on living (or working!) forever, "then an ounce of prevention is worth a pound of cure." You are best served by engaging wealth management professionals to help make the process simple, easy, and *effective*.

Of course, you **could** work with individual professionals in all these areas (legal, accounting, tax, etc.) You may even believe you already have a plan for each of these areas.

Warning

But there's a potential pitfall to that approach of which you must be aware. When working with many disparate individuals, you could end up subject to conflicting and sometimes incomplete advice.

The Result?

You end up making essentially "random" investment, insurance, tax, trust, business succession planning, and estate planning decisions that are all in isolation of each other. This will lead to a collection of investments, insurance, business, and trust structures that are fragmented, confusing, and not particularly tax efficient. When this happens, you become vulnerable to missed opportunities, unnecessary expenses, and unforeseen tax liabilities. It's not an exaggeration to say that the consequences could be catastrophic.

That's why an *integrated* transition plan is necessary. It's the only way to ensure everything is done right and nothing is missed.

There's another reason to hire a professional transition team to assist you. You see, some business owners never *really* retire, especially if they have transitioned the business to their children. They still keep an eye on how the business is run because they want to make sure their retirement remains secure. This creates a lot of stress both on the business owner and on his/her children. The business owner can't let things go, and the children can't make decisions for themselves.

Here's the good news. With an experienced transition team, you don't have to keep a never-ending eye on your business, because you don't have to worry about keeping your retirement secure. By working with a team to create a transition plan, you'll be able to extract enough assets from your business to set up a separate retirement portfolio *before* you ever quit working. And you'll have increased confidence that your retirement is secure.

How Can You Find That Experienced Advisor?

Let's first talk about wealth and wealth management.

What Is Wealth Management and Why Should You Care?

Wealth management is more than just investment advice.

Wealth management encompasses all parts of a person's personal and business life. A person's wealth is not just what they have in their investment portfolio – it's everything they have accumulated: their home, their cottage, their business, other business interests, investment property, etc.

To manage all these assets requires the advice of multiple professionals from accountants, lawyers, investment advisors, realtors, bankers, mortgage brokers, insurance agents, financial planners, estate planners and many more.

Most of these advisors usually work in isolation of each other. This isolation can result in conflicting and sometimes incomplete advice, leading to bad financial decisions that happen in isolation of a person's overall financial objectives and needs.

The reality is, while most people have an investment plan, an insurance plan, a tax plan, and maybe even a business succession plan and/or estate plan, these plans were most likely done for them at different times by different advisors in isolation of each other.

The result is a collection of investments, insurance, business and trust structures that are fragmented and not tax-efficient, resulting in missed opportunities, and unnecessary expense, unforeseen tax liability, duplication of obligations and at worst, catastrophic consequences.

Rather than trying to make sense of the sometimes-conflicting advice from these professionals, business families can benefit from a holistic approach to managing their wealth with a single advisor who coordinates all the services they need to manage their wealth and plan for their own and/or their family's current and future needs.

Wealth Advisors start by developing a plan that will grow and protect their clients' wealth based on their clients' personal financial situation, goals, comfort level, risk tolerance and needs.

This would encompass an investment plan to manage their investments, a risk plan to manage the risks to their wealth and livelihood, a personal tax plan to manage the tax implications of managing their personal wealth, a business tax and succession plan to plan the sale or transition of their business to new owners when they retire in a tax-efficient manner, and an estate plan to transfer their assets to the next generation tax-efficiently that also meets their wishes on who gets what and how.

Once all these plans are created, the wealth advisor works with their clients' own network of professionals to implement the various components of their plan and then meets with them on a regular basis to review and monitor the progress of their plans.

These plans are revised and updated when needed. Wealth Advisors touch every aspect of their clients' wealth from growing, protecting, and transferring their wealth to the next generation.

Most financial advisors are not Wealth Advisors. They do not have the knowledge or access to integrated wealth management services.

So how do you find a Wealth Advisor that can offer all the services mentioned above?

Good question!

Let's talk about the **7 Key Questions Every Financial Advisor MUST Be Able to Answer** before you hire them to manage your wealth so that you can achieve financial freedom, security and peace of mind!

Now... you may be expecting a series of questions like:

"Do you have any samples of the types of portfolios you recommend?"

"What are your fees?"

"Can you show me testimonials?"

"How are your fees charged?"

"What is your track record?"

And all those are good questions. Any financial advisor worth their salt will have ready responses in place.

As someone who has been there in the trenches with the best of them, let me lay on you some queries the average financial advisor ISN'T expecting... which will enable you to see who's ready to advise you on your money and family wealth.

Ok here we go...

I have prepared a list of questions that you can ask. To access these questions, go to **www.7keyquestions.ca**

DOWNLOAD MY FREE BOOK

Do you have the right financial advisor working for you? Not sure?

Find out in my new book:

Who's Investing Your Money?–

Learn How to Ask the Right Questions to Select the Best Financial Advisor for Your Situation

To get your free book visit:
www.whosinvestingyourmoney.com

In this next section I will be discussing some specific issues in some detail to demonstrate the wealth and breadth of knowledge required to effectively structure the business transition.

Feel free to contact me for specifics.
(604) 855-6846

CHAPTER 14

SELLING YOUR BUSINESS

Essentially, you have two basic options for exiting your business.

1. The **first** is to sell to another person or another business owner. It's an arms-length transaction, and as such will often require the most effort and discipline. But it's also the option that usually provides the highest financial reward. These days, however, many business owners don't end up choosing to sell their businesses. Instead, they take the second option.

2. The **second** – and more common – option is to transfer or sell your business to the next generation of your family.

Management expert Peter Drucker, perhaps a little tongue in cheek, calls this **"the final test of greatness"** for business leaders.

Family dynamics make this choice arguably the most complex, and studies show this transfer to be successful in only around 30% of cases.[1]

Just 10% of businesses successfully reach the 3rd generation![2] However, the right amount of openness, clarity and respect between family members, along with legally sound transfer/sale documents, will go a long way towards making this option a great triumph.

---

[1] Family Business Institute http://www.familybusinessinstitute.com/index.php/succession-planning/

[2] Family Business Institute http://www.familybusinessinstitute.com/index.php/succession-planning/

CHAPTER 15

TAX STRATEGIES FOR BUSINESS OWNERS

In this chapter, I will make some broad observations.

As with the other subjects discussed, your mileage may vary.

This too will be an introduction and should not be construed as giving tax advice. That is best left to tax lawyers and business tax specialists.

Tax strategies deserve special consideration for two very broad reasons.

The **first** is the tax-saving advantages that can be gained by planning properly long before you sell your business.

The **second** reason is the not-so-pleasant tax repercussions that will occur should you sell or transition your business improperly, particularly under the watchful eyes of the CRA (Canada Revenue Agency).

Fortunately, business owners have several options when it comes to minimizing the tax consequences of selling or transitioning their business. Here are two important ones to know:

Capital Gains Exemption

This is perhaps the most popular tax planning technique.

With a Capital Gains Exemption, or CGE, you can sell qualified shares of a qualified small business corporation (QSBC) and earn an exemption from having to pay a capital gains tax on the gains of up to $800,000 per spouse or individual family member on the sale of the shares owned by family members of a family owned (QSBC).

Note: Advanced planning is required for your children to qualify.

To qualify for the Capital Gains Exemption, certain conditions apply. For example, if your corporation has excess cash or assets that are not actively being used in the daily operation of the business, this may disqualify you from being eligible.

Also, if some of your business assets do not qualify, steps will need to be taken to ensure that the business qualifies. This can take years to do, meaning you should plan now to ensure all of your assets qualify.

Every business and business owner is unique, and so is each business owner's tax situation.

Also, see my comments about tax implications of separation or divorce in Chapter 5.

A Wealth Advisor will have an army of experts available to help you navigate the dangerous waters of the Tax Code.

Here are three examples of how wealth advisors are valuable allies in the fight to reduce taxes and how to deal with conflicting advice from various advisors.

Example 1

As they neared retirement, a couple wanted to divest their interest in a business. The company balance sheet had some anomalies and they agreed to a review by a tax lawyer and an accountant.

Canadian shareholders are entitled to a one-time $800,000 lifetime capital gains exemption if their company qualifies as a Qualified Small Business Corporation (QSBC). The criteria for businesses are rigorous and if they are unable to meet the criteria the tax implications are serious.

The lawyer mentioned the company was looking at a tax liability of $250,000 for failing to meet the criteria.

The accountant discovered that the couple's partners owned a holding company with a $450,000 insurance policy on each of the partners with the partners being direct beneficiaries of the policies. Since the policies were owned by the company and the premiums were paid by the company these policies posed a significant tax liability. Should either of the insured die, the insured's estate would receive the proceeds and the proceeds would be taxable to the deceased's estate. The potential tax liability was approximately $220,000 for each partner.

To rectify this potential tax liability, the company was named the beneficiary rather than either partner. Should a partner die, the insurance proceeds would then be received by the company tax-free and be paid out as a dividend to the surviving shareholder tax-free through the corporation's capital dividend account.

Soon after the changes one of the partners passed away and the spouse received the full $450,000 insurance proceeds tax-free, saving her almost $220,000 in taxes.

The Lifetime Capital Gains exemption and the insurance policy restructuring meant total tax savings of $470,000.

These real-life examples help illustrate the importance of comprehensive and integrated wealth management plan utilizing professionals who work together to understand your complete financial picture.

Why send the government money when you and your family can make much better use of it?

Good advisors can and will make a difference in your financial health and wealth.

Example 2

For over 15 years, a businessman resisted undertaking a detailed financial plan and financial check-up. Finally, when he took ill, he relented and provided all his financial documents (personal and business).

I had a tax lawyer review the legal documents. The lawyer noted the client was bequeathing his wife $500,000 and a life interest in the family home in his will as well as an additional $500,000 from a trust. She would receive a total of $1,000,000 and the family home.

In discussion, the client indicated his wife was to receive the home and only $500,000. The misunderstanding arose when a second, different lawyer set up an Alter-Ego Trust at the request of the accountant to protect the client's personal assets from his estate. This included a provision for an additional $500,000 from the trust as well.

A simple correction resolved this misunderstanding and the beneficiary once again stood to receive a life interest in the home and only $500,000.

This is an example of how important it is to have competent professionals available to assess your complete financial picture.

It's true that not all financial plans are this complex, but having access to a team that can deliver answers to complex problems is a welcome change.

Example 3

A retired farm couple owned a holding company that held the proceeds from the sale of their farm quota. By claiming their personal lifetime capital gains exemptions, they were able to extract capital out of their holding company. However, they still had approximately $550,000 remaining in their holding company.

Their children had no interest in taking over the farm so the money could not be rolled over to their children. The couple had significant assets outside of their holding company, so there was no need to withdraw money from the holding company to maintain their lifestyle.

My clients wanted to wind down the holding company as it was a dead asset as far as they were concerned and a potentially significant tax liability to their children.

With a life expectancy of over 15 years, the couple saw that their assets would easily grow to over $1,000,000.

Years ago, the farm couple had purchased a $500,000 joint last-to-die insurance policy as an estate planning tool to reduce personal taxes on their death.

I had an insurance expert review their policies.

Upon reviewing their current tax situation and seeing the couple wanted to reduce the estate tax liability of their holding company, the insurance expert recommended a tax-free asset transfer.

The couple would sell their personal policy to their corporation. We had an actuary review their policy to determine the current market value of the policy. Based on their age and health, it was determined that the policy was worth approximately $250,000. This meant that they would receive approximately $250,000 from their corporation by selling the policy to the company. When they pass away, the proceeds from the insurance policy would be received by the corporation and passed through the Capital Dividend account tax-free to their beneficiaries.

The couple incurred some personal taxes on the gain in value between the time they purchased the insurance policy to when they sold it to their company, but the tax liability was minimal and the tax-free benefit was substantial.

CHAPTER 16

ENOUGH FOR YOU AND YOUR FAMILY'S FUTURE

An important part of the transition process is to create a comprehensive plan encompassing all aspects of your financial life. By understanding what specifically about money is important to you, and how much you will need to achieve your goals, dreams, and lifestyle needs, you will have a better idea of when work can become optional for you instead of mandatory. This also helps give you the peace of mind you need in order to ensure you are exercising sound judgment when the time comes to sell or transition your business.

Whenever you *do* decide to retire, it's critical that you have sufficient assets to provide a secure future for yourself and your family. There are a lot of factors to consider when it comes to this step, but there are two in particular that should be near the top of every list:

Income and Expenses

Why are these two so important?

To put it bluntly, it all comes down to this simple rule. *You cannot retire successfully unless your income is **more** than your outgo.*

It sounds like a no-brainer, and it is. Yet I can't count the number of people I meet every week who have no idea what their income will be after their retirement… never mind if it will be more than their expenses. These people want to retire; they hope to retire, but they don't know if they really can.

Of course, there's more to retiring successfully than just being able to pay the bills.

Retirement is all about finally having the time and opportunity to try new things, go new places, and learn new skills. Here again is why income is so important. All those things cost money. So how do you know what you can do after retirement if you don't know whether you'll have the money to do it?

This is what you need to do. First, sit down and calculate what your income and expenses are *now*. Here are some questions you need to answer.

What is your monthly income after taxes?

How much do you pay in monthly utilities?

How much debt do you have, and what are your monthly payments like? Remember, this can include mortgage payments, car payments, credit card payments, etc.

How much do you spend on automobile insurance, home insurance, gas, and other regular expenses? Don't forget to consider any out-of-pocket medical costs.

Step 1:

Once you've tallied those numbers, subtract your expenses from your income. Whatever number remains is what's immediately available to set aside for retirement.

Now determine what expenses might change after retirement. For example:

What expenses will you have more difficulty paying once you are no longer drawing regular income from your business?

What expenses do you currently have that will *decrease* after retirement?

What is your current tax bracket? Will it change after you retire and start earning less income?

Now comes the home stretch.

Finish these final steps:

Step 2:

Take your existing expenses then add the expenses that will go *up* after retirement. Next, subtract the expenses that will go *down*. Hold on to that number for a moment.

Step 3:

Calculate the amount of income you expect to receive from Canada Pension Plan (CPP), Old Age Security (OAS) and any retirement accounts you have, like a Registered Retirement Savings Plan (RRSP), investment accounts, or Tax-Free Savings Account (TFSA). Then subtract the tax you'll owe on these accounts once you start using them.

But remember; the order in which you draw income from these accounts is very important, because it will have a significant impact on how much net income you will receive in retirement and how long your retirement income will last.

You also need to consider the effect of inflation on your income and expenses. You may think you have enough when you retire. However, you must factor in the official average annual rate of inflation, which is 2%.

In addition, retirees often find that their personal rate of inflation is much higher. Also, be sure to factor in a realistic rate of return on your retirement investments, or you may find after 20 years of retirement that you do not have enough to achieve all your retirement goals. The good news is that we can show you how long your money will last with inflation calculated into your plan.

Take the final number from Step 3 and combine it with the amount you can save from Step 1. Then compare it to the number from Step 2. Steps 1 and 3 combined is your income after retirement. Step 2 is your expenses.

Which number is higher?

Keep in mind that every number you reach from this exercise is just a loose estimate. Too loose, in fact, to make financial decisions by, but at the very least, this should get you thinking. And if you'd like a much more concrete projection of your income and expenses after retirement, all you have to do is give me a call.

Helping people plan for retirement is my specialty. I'd be happy to sit down with you, ask some questions, and prepare a comprehensive estimate.

Just contact me at (604) 855-6846 and we can schedule a time to meet.

In the meantime, just remember this fundamental truth: ***you cannot retire successfully unless your income is more than your expenses.*** Remember, too, that your income should be enough to cover your wants as well as your needs. So, start thinking about it today. It's a complex topic, but you've got plenty of time if you start working on it now.

To sum up, creating a formal business transition plan should provide you with a blueprint of *what* your goals in life will cost, *how* to be able to afford them, and *when* to execute various strategies designed to help you achieve them.

CHAPTER 17

PREPARING YOUR FAMILY

Preparing your family for a smooth and efficient transition

Have you ever heard of the "**Six W**" questions? They go like this: **Who, What, When, Where, Why,** and **How.** If you are planning on transitioning your business to a member (or members) of your family, each of these questions will need to be answered…and it's important that your family be involved. Too often, business owners make all the decisions by themselves, springing them on family members at the last minute. This can lead to mistakes, stress, and resentment…and ultimately, to a failing business.

Answering the "**Six W**" questions isn't easy, but fortunately, you don't have to do it alone. While I focus mainly on the *financial* aspects of transitioning your business, there are professionals out there who specialize in the family and emotional aspects.

Please contact me if you have questions about the family and emotional aspects of business transition.

CHAPTER 18

HOW CAN I HELP YOU?

Our Family Business Transition Process

Helping family businesses create the kind of business transition plan described above is my goal. I do this through the 8-step process outlined earlier.

Business owners who dream of retiring someday, are encouraged to sit down with me to discuss their business transition plan.

Here's How It Works

The moment you walk through my door you'll be treated like a client. I'll have a cup of coffee, or tea, waiting if you want it. When we sit down together, my philosophy is first to *listen* rather than speak.

I want to know about your goals, your dreams, your needs. What do you want to do with your business? What do you want to protect? It's my job to learn these details. Only then will I suggest a possible course of action.

In this way, we can help you **visualize** your desired future. Then, we'll take stock of what you have to work with and what obstacles need to be overcome to reach that future.

We'll examine and list all your **Strengths, Weaknesses, Opportunities,** and **Threats (SWOT)**. This is how we **analyze your current reality**.

From here, business owners can decide whether they truly want to **commit to creating a plan**. Because they now have a greater understanding of what they want *and* what they have to overcome, we find at this point that most business owners are more excited and motivated to create a plan than ever before.

For any transition to be effective, however, business owners first need to ensure they have a **solid wealth foundation** on which to retire. This is why we recommend that business owners take advantage of our **Integrated Wealth Management** services through Assante Private Client, a division of CI Private Counsel LP.

Integrated Wealth Management

"Integrated Wealth Management" means combining *every* aspect of your financial life into an overall plan.

This involves four main aspects:
- Your investment selections
- Your asset allocation
- Your taxes
- Your estate

Some business owners may have a few investments here and there, or have had their taxes looked at by a professional, or filled out a will several years ago. But most business owners don't have a plan in place for *all* these things.

Business owners who enlist my services, enjoy having each of these aspects working *in concert* together rather than separately. For example, doesn't it make more sense to know how your investments will affect your taxes, and vice versa? Doesn't it make more sense to factor in how your *heirs'* taxes will be impacted when your estate is passed onto them?

The fact of the matter is that most of your wealth is tied up in your business. Selling or transitioning your business will have a major impact on your overall wealth.

That's why it's so important to integrate every aspect of your wealth into your plan. It's the only way to ensure said impact will be positive instead of negative. Furthermore, once you have sold or transitioned your business, you will need to have an investment strategy in place to better manage the proceeds from the sale, or the lump sum you extracted from the business to secure your retirement.

Many business owners like to keep a constant eye on the business even after they have technically handed off the day-to-day management duties. This is because they want to make sure their retirement remains secure.

By having an Integrated Wealth Management Plan in place, you'll be able to spend more time *enjoying* retirement and less time worrying about it. That's because your plan will likely recommend setting aside sufficient assets into a separate retirement account *outside* of your business before retirement.

This is your retirement nest egg. More importantly, your plan will specify how much "sufficient" actually is. This way, once your account is large enough, you'll be able to generate income *before* you retire from your business.

You know what that means: greater peace of mind. With your own retirement secure, you can more readily forego the daily grind and let your heirs run the business and make decisions for themselves.

Ultimately, having an Integrated Wealth Management Plan means enjoying the fruits of your hard-earned labor, while your children begin making decisions on their own.

To put it simply, participating in our Integrated Wealth Management program will enable you to have a **solid wealth foundation** on which to retire.

Your Business Transition Plan

Once your wealth foundation is in place, we can then **design a specific, personal transition plan for you**. During this process, we will connect with any other professionals you are already working with – attorneys, accountants, etc. – to create the simplest, most direct path from where you are to where you want to be.

Remember, your plan should help you:
1. Determine the value of your business
2. Find the right buyer
3. Choose the right time to sell
4. Decide whether to transition your business to a family member or sell to a non-related party

5. Determine whether selling your business will bring in enough proceeds to fund your retirement and other financial goals.
6. Ensure the orderly payment and transition of ownership/management of your business to your successor/heir.
7. Minimize the taxes that come from selling your business
8. Ensure you have sufficient assets to secure you and your family's future

Once your plan is created, it will be time to **execute your plan**. But the responsibility shouldn't fall on your shoulders alone – we'll be there to hold your hand through the entire process. We do that by meeting regularly with you to review your plan and assess your progress. We will also work closely with your legal and accounting teams to implement all the financial, legal, insurance, and tax strategies your plan contains.

Then comes the best part. Executing your plan will enable you to reach your destination. To **achieve your desired future**. Even then, however, our work is not done. We'll meet with you every three-to-six months, or more often if necessary, to check in on how you're doing. We'll also document any major changes in your financial situation that require us to adjust your plan.

Finally, we will assist you with the eighth and final step of the Business Transition Process, which is to **share your family's wealth**. By this point, you have built a solid wealth foundation, sold or transferred your business, and achieved your desired future. In this final step, we continue to meet with you *and* your heirs on an as-needed basis to ensure that your family's future – and your legacy – endures for generations to come.

Our Clients

If you are interested in learning more about our Business Transition Process and Integrated Wealth Management Services, I'd love to hear from you!

In our experience, the services we offer work best with certain types of business families. That's why our clients are part of a select group of business families with a certain net worth who have decided to invest a portion of their assets with Assante Private Client. Assante Private Client is a division of CI Private Counsel LP, which houses the Wealth Planning Group.

Of course, whether you choose to become a client or not, it's always a good idea to at least come in for a free consultation. Together, we can help you understand some of your options and which path is best for you. From there, you can decide whether or not to continue with our planning process by becoming an investment client.

Learn more about how Assante can help you grow, preserve, and protect your retirement assets, please call me at (604) 855-6846 or email me at **aspitters@assante.com**.

Summary

It should be clear by now that to reach your retirement goals, it may become necessary to sell your business someday.

To sell your business in a timely, cost-effective, and *profitable* manner, you need to have a business transition plan.

It's this plan that will give you the step by step instructions needed to ensure the orderly transition of your business to your buyer and/or your heirs, minimize taxes, and ensure you have sufficient assets for both you and your family's future.

CHAPTER 19

HOW DO YOU START THE PROCESS?

Do Not Do It Alone!

The world of finance has gotten more complex than ever. It takes years of time and training to master all the intricacies of financial planning, to say nothing of the laws and regulations that seem to change every year.

As a business owner, your time and energy should be spent on one thing: your business.

That's why it's so crucial to choose an experienced, qualified wealth management expert to help you. Such an expert can answer your questions and look closely at your business before suggesting the best course of action. An expert can do the legwork and manage your plan, giving you confidence and peace of mind.

To demonstrate what a business transition plan would look like, and how it would fit within our overall **Integrated Wealth Management services**, I'm currently offering a free consultation to business owners in Fraser Valley.

If you are reading this book in another province and want to meet with an Assante Advisor, I can arrange an introduction for you.

All we'll do is sit down, have a cup of coffee, and look at your goals and needs. I'll explain some of the things you'll need to consider and where to get started. There's no obligation on your part. If you need further assistance from me, I'd be thrilled to provide it. If not, no matter. I'm just happy to help in any way I can!

If you want to take me up on my offer, just give me a call at (604) 855-6846, or e-mail me at **aspitters@assante.com.** We'll set up a time to meet whenever is most convenient for you. Keep in mind that the sooner we meet, the sooner you can have a plan in place. And remember…

If your goal is to quit working someday, creating a plan is a must.

Thinking about your future is a must.

Taking action is a must, too.

Don't waste another day. Start now!

Call me today: (604) 855-6846

CHAPTER 20

ADRIAN SPITTERS AND ASSANTE

Wealth Planning Group

Your Business. Your Family. Your Future.

The Wealth Planning Group of Assante Private Client provides Integrated Wealth Management Solutions to Canadian business families in the areas of ***tax planning, retirement planning, and wealth transfer***. My association with Assante Wealth Management gives me access to this group, which is comprised of lawyers, accountants, financial analysts, insurance experts, business succession planning and estate planning professionals.

Taxation represents the single largest expense and loss of capital in the lives of many business families, particularly in the retirement phase. The wealth planning group and I work directly with the business family to help them understand the complex tax and financial issues that need to be addressed to minimize loss of business wealth when important transitions or transactions occur.

Tax, Financial and Estate Planning

As a Wealth Advisor, my main focus and strengths are tax minimization, wealth planning and estate planning, including:
- Planning for the tax efficient transfer of the family business to the next generation;
- Pre-retirement planning for the tax-efficient sale of the business inventory and other assets;
- Planning tax efficient business structures for the family business and other ventures;
- Personal tax and estate planning;
- Financial and retirement planning.

My approach is to bring together not only tax, estate and financial planning, but also tax efficient managed wealth solutions and insurance strategies, all personalized to meet the unique needs and values of each client family.

Coordinating Professional Advice

The busy lives of business families can seem further complicated by the necessary involvement of professionals from various disciplines, such as accountants and lawyers. The Wealth Planning Group provides a comprehensive plan that coordinates the services of these professionals. The Wealth Planning Group creates the plan, helps coordinate its implementation with the client family's accountant and lawyer, and continues to monitor the client family's tax and financial affairs thereafter and through the retirement years.

Initial Introduction

As a Wealth Advisor, I provide a free initial consultation to introduce our wealth management program and to review your investment portfolio and financial situation for opportunities and income tax strategies.

What You Can Expect

- Comprehensive financial planning encompassing tax, insurance, estate, and succession planning based on your long-term goals while still providing for the short-term needs of you and your family
- A personal investment plan based on your goals, tax situation, income requirements, and risk tolerance
- Access to tax lawyers, accountants, and insurance, estate and investment specialists
- Identification, explanation and coordination of tax and estate planning strategies to be implemented by your professional advisors
- Ongoing monitoring of your investments and regular reviews of your financial, tax, and estate plans

A Commitment to Business Families

I am committed to maintaining the high levels of proficiency and expertise required to provide professional advice.

READY TO SELL YOUR BUSINESS?

Adrian Spitters •

Senior Wealth Advisor •

Assante Capital Management Ltd.

604 - 855 - 6846 •

aspitters@assante.com

Web: www.businesstransitionadvisor.ca

CHAPTER 21

BUSINESS WEALTH PLANNING CHECKLIST

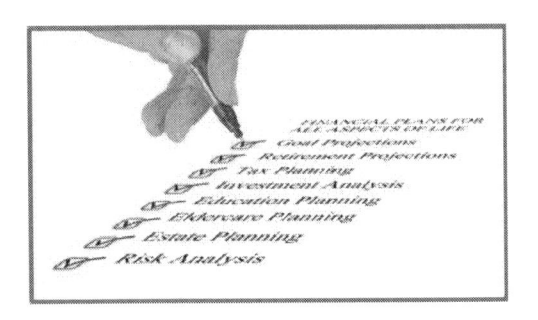

Here is a sample Business Wealth Planning Check List

Wealth planning is more than investment returns

It is a process to maximize what you have, provide for your future and effectively pass it on.

Wealth planning is not just for the "wealthy"

It is something that everyone should do. It is never too early or too late to plan.

Wealth planning provides a financial framework for your life and beyond.

It is personal. It is customised. And it works.

BIG PICTURE

My 3 biggest concerns today are:

1. _____

_____

_____

2. _____

_____

_____

3. _____

_____

_____

READY TO SELL YOUR BUSINESS?

What are your most important planning objectives	NOT Important	Important	VERY Important
Identifying all the issues you need to consider: financial, retirement, tax, succession or sale issues			
Having enough money to sustain your desired lifestyle in retirement			
Structuring your affairs to minimize tax now, at retirement and on death			
Maximizing returns in your investment portfolio			
Deciding whether/when you will be ready for a change in lifestyle			
Passing the business to your child(ren) while balancing non-business child(ren)'s interests			
Taking care of others in the event of your illness, disability or death - parents, children, grandchildren			
Leaving a personal legacy - values, traditions, ethics, life lessons and inheritance			
Paying for children's or grandchildren's education			
Maximizing a gift/bequest to your favorite charity			
Avoiding probate fees			
Avoiding family conflict after you're gone			

Retirement Planning	NOT Important	Important	VERY Important
Do you know when you can financially afford to retire?			
Do you have a plan for when, or if, you will retire from active business & a clear vision of your life in retirement?			
Do you and your spouse agree on what your lifestyle will be in retirement?			
Do you know how much you need to receive on an after-tax basis from the sale of your business to enable you to maintain your current lifestyle in retirement?			
Do you know how much you can spend monthly/annually during retirement without outliving savings?			
Do you sometimes wonder if it is important to diversify some wealth into some non-business assets?			
Do you wonder if completely eliminating all income tax every year might not be the best retirement planning?			
Do you think you can minimize current taxes and also save for retirement at the same time?			
Do you know how to hold retirement savings so they don't interfere with business tax planning opportunities?			
Do you know how many years in advance a business owner must start planning for retirement?			

READY TO SELL YOUR BUSINESS?

Retirement Planning	NOT Important	Important	VERY Important
Do you know why is it harder for a business owner to defer income in the years leading up to retirement?			
Will you need to rely on government pension for income? * should you apply for CPP early? * will your OAS benefits be subject to the claw back?			
Do you know which retirement income sources to spend first and how to minimize taxes?			
Do you review your financial plan regularly?			
Do you know the minimum rate of return required on your investments to ensure you have enough?			

Tax Planning	NOT Important	Important	VERY Important
Are you sure you are currently minimizing unnecessary exposure to tax?			
Are you minimizing personal taxes on non-business assets such as investments?			
Do you have a strategy in place to minimize the income tax you pay on your investments?			
Are you in a structure that enables you to withdraw funds from your portfolio on a tax-free basis?			

Tax Planning	NOT Important	Important	VERY Important
Does your portfolio give you exposure to underlying securities that produce a mixture of interest, foreign income, Canadian dividends and capital gains, but return on investment is ultimately taxed preferentially as Canadian dividends and/or capital gains?			
Are you maximizing any and all income splitting opportunities available to you, with your spouse or children, or even through a corporate structure or a family trust?			
Do you know which assets can be rolled over tax free to your spouse and which assets will be subject to tax at death?			
Do you know how much of your lifetime Capital Gains Exemption (CGE) you have left and are you certain which assets are CGE eligible?			
If you are a proprietor (not partnership or corporation), do you understand: * how to minimize tax exposure on business income? * how a business partnership could create tax savings? * how incorporating the operation could save tax in the years leading to retirement?			

READY TO SELL YOUR BUSINESS?

Tax Planning	NOT Important	Important	VERY Important
If you are a proprietor (not partnership or corporation):			
* Are you confident you are minimizing tax exposure on business income?			
* Do you know how a business partnership could create tax savings?			
* Do you understand how incorporating the business operation could save tax now and in the years leading up to retirement?			
If you operate your business through a corporation:			
* Are you confident you are minimizing your corporate tax bill?			
* Do you know if your shares will qualify for the lifetime capital gains exemption (CGE)?			
* Does your corporate structure ensure that your shares will always qualify for the lifetime capital gains exemption (CGE) in the event of your death?			
* Have you obtained advice about whether you need a separate holding corporation?			
* Does your business succession plan provide for the most tax effective transfer of shares to family members?			

Tax Planning	NOT Important	Important	VERY Important
*` Do you understand how corporately held insurance can create a tax efficient succession plan? * Do you know if you are maximizing access to the lowest corporate tax rate?			
Does your current corporate structure: * maximize income splitting opportunities with your family members on an annual basis· * on the sale of your business and on your death? (i.e. ability to split income with them through the payment of dividends currently and subsequent to client's death and to utilize their capital gains exemption on the potential share sale of their business)			
If you own shares in a small business corporation, have you obtained advice about whether or not your business will qualify for the capital gains exemption in the event of a share sale?			
Do you have a formal business succession plan / exit strategy in place?			

Tax Planning	NOT Important	Important	VERY Important
If you have multiple shareholders in your business, do you have a shareholders' agreement? * If you have a shareholders' agreement, does it provide for a tax efficient exit from your business on retirement, disagreement, death or disability? * Does the shareholders' agreement adequately protect your family in the event of your death or does it favour the remaining shareholders? * Does the shareholders' agreement clearly outline how the value of your shares will be determined on death, disability and retirement?			
Have you reviewed what the tax savings could be by holding any existing personally owned life insurance through your corporation rather than in your personal names?			
Is your corporate structure set up to minimize exposure to your business' creditors, in particular, if you have significant cash or investment assets inside your corporation(s)?			

ESTATE PLANNING	NOT Important	Important	VERY Important
Do you know: * how taxes will affect your estate * how much your estate will pay in probate fees			
Do you know how tax will impact your: * non-registered investments? * registered assets (RRSP's, RRIF's)? * other assets such as real estate?			
Do you understand how the capital gains exemption applies at death?			
Have you completed a recent inventory of: * assets of significant value? * personal effects? * tems of emotional value?			
Do you know the difference between "joint tenancy" and "tenancy in common" and the reasons for using the various ownership methods?			
Have you made, or do intend on making gifts during your lifetime?			
Do you have a current will?			

ESTATE PLANNING

ESTATE PLANNING	NOT Important	Important	VERY Important
Have you specifically discussed your estate plan with your family?			
Have you specifically discussed your intentions regarding your business with your children?			
Have you obtained advice about ways to create a "fair" distribution of estate value as between business and non-business children?			
Do you have any concerns about: * how your beneficiaries will manage and/or spend their inheritance? * whether a marriage breakdown could put your child's inheritance at risk? * how your family will deal with the family cottage?			
Do you know all the uses of trusts and how they can benefit you and your beneficiaries?			
Do you understand how trusts can save income tax?			
Do you understand how trusts can protect your children from marriage breakdown or creditor claims?			

ESTATE PLANNING	NOT Important	Important	VERY Important
Have you selected: 　* an Executor and alternate Executor? 　* a guardian for minor children? 　* a Power of Attorney for financial and property matters? 　* a Power of Attorney for end of life decisions?			
Does your current will reflect your family's current circumstances and current wishes or does it need to be updated?			
Is your will drafted to minimize potential family conflict upon your death?			
Have you included long-term trusts in your will planning for income tax savings for your beneficiaries on their inheritance?			
Does your will help protect your beneficiaries' inheritances from potential matrimonial and creditor claims? (i.e. Is this a reason to incorporate testamentary trusts?)			
Do you want to be able to control the use and timing of your child's inheritance after your death? (i.e. Is this a reason to incorporate testamentary trusts?)			
If you plan for some but not all of your children to take over your business, have you devised a plan to treat all children equitably (presuming this is your intention)?			

READY TO SELL YOUR BUSINESS?

ESTATE PLANNING	NOT Important	Important	VERY Important
Are you in a second marriage, and if so, does your will ensure your current spouse and any children from your previous marriage are provided for consistent with your wishes?			

RISK MANAGEMENT	NOT Important	Important	VERY Important
Do you know what the tax liability will be on the second to die of you and your spouse?			
Are there sufficient liquid assets available to fund this liability without forcing the sale of your illiquid assets such as your business and real estate?			
Have you explored ways to minimize this tax cost on your death? (i.e. either funding with insurance or potentially considering an estate freeze in favour of your children)			
Have you obtained tax advice on potential exposure to U.S. estate tax on your death?			
Do you know if you have too much or too little insurance in place to ensure your family's financial security in the event of your premature death? (i.e. income replacement insurance)			

List below any issues you want to discuss with:

1. Family Members:

_____

_____

_____

2. Partners or Shareholders in Your Business:

_____

_____

_____

3. Your Financial Advisor:

_____

_____

_____

In the following Chapters
I would like to talk about selecting
a good financial or wealth advisor.

Getting this right
means you are well on your way
to preserving and growing your wealth.

CHAPTER 22

WHAT TYPE OF ADVISOR SHOULD I CHOOSE?

Why is this important?

Two Main Reasons:

REASON #1

If you hire or are working with a financial advisor who does not take a holistic approach to managing your wealth, you may be working with an advisor who does not see the big financial picture in your life and only will advise within their core competency.

They may shy away from giving you advice or directing you to someone who can give you advice on other areas of your financial life critically important to your financial well-being.

REASON #2

Families may be getting incomplete advice.

If you HIRE or are working with an advisor who does not or cannot offer an integrated approach to managing your wealth, you will need to work with additional advisors to get a complete picture of your overall wealth.

Coordinating the advice from multiple advisors can be a challenge.

When you work with multiple advisors to provide advice on the various aspects of your financial life, you will find that they may not necessarily communicate with each other to get a full understanding of your overall investment strategy and financial goals.

As a result, they may offer conflicting and sometimes incomplete investment, tax, trust, business succession and estate planning advice.

You may be making financial decisions that happen in isolation of your overall investment objectives and financial needs. The result is a collection of investments that are **fragmented, expensive, not very tax-efficient and not doing as well as you expected.**

Aren't All Financial Advisors the Same?

A wide range of differences exist between the expertise and services offered by the various types of financial advisors.

Not knowing what these differences are and hiring the wrong financial advisor can be harmful to your financial health. A financial advisor is a professional who renders financial services to clients. The terms such as financial advisor and financial specialist maybe general terms or job titles used by investment professionals and do not denote any specific designations.

When evaluating investment advisors, selecting the advisor with the lowest fee possible may not always be the most prudent decision.

A wealth advisor or financial planner offering the services of private wealth management can offer a full range of services for the same fee you may already be paying your stock broker or mutual fund advisor.

When the fees charged are embedded (hidden), as they are in many mutual funds, the investor often mistakenly believes the service is free.

When the fee is charged separately or is disclosed, and the investor only receives investment advice, this advice becomes a commodity.

As a result, the only difference between advisors is the size of the advisors' fee.

The best way to evaluate advisors is by asking the 7 questions mentioned in Chapter 13.

You as a smart investor will find it much easier to evaluate their level of service and determine whether their fees match their level of service.

CHAPTER 23

WHAT CAN I EXPECT IN TERMS OF FEES

Advisors are paid for their services in three ways:
1. Commissions
2. Fee-based – Combination of commission and fee only
3. Fee-only

1. Stock brokers and mutual fund salespeople make money when they sell a stock or a fund.

1.1   Stock brokers receive a transaction fee or a flat fee for each stock or bond they put into your account.

1.2   The fees for mutual funds are called loads and are charged:
- when your advisor buys a fund
- when your advisor sells a fund (the full commission is charged if sold in the first year and declines every year thereafter to $0, typically after 7 years) or
- on an annual basis (a flat fee based on **Assets Under Management** (AUM)).

2. Fee-based advisors may receive both fees and commissions. They will charge fees based on Assets Under Management (AUM) for their financial/investment planning services and receive commissions for the products they recommend as well.

Total management fees can thus range from 1.50% to as high as 3.5% when you combine both investment advisor fees and mutual fund manager fees.

3. Fee-only advisors are paid directly by their clients and do not receive commissions or fees based on **Assets Under Management.** This fee can be a flat retainer fee or an hourly rate. The hourly or retainer fee can vary widely based on advisor experience and complexity of a client's financial affairs.

Some people ask, "Why should I pay you for the services my commission advisor does for free?" **They believe, incorrectly, that commission advisors are not being paid by the client.**

Recall that the advisor is indeed being compensated either by commission or transaction fee for brokers or by having the mutual fund company deduct the fee from the investments or by charging a fee directly.

One important factor to consider is that for the same fee (or commission) that you pay a stock broker or mutual fund representative to buy and sell stocks and funds, you can receive comprehensive, investment and wealth planning from a full-service Wealth Advisor who is backed by an Investment Management Team.

The fee you pay, either embedded or visible, should be based on the value you receive. If the advice given is just pure investment advice, then the fee should be lower.

If the advice includes an investment policy statement, financial planning, retirement planning, estate planning, tax planning or integrated wealth management, the fee should reflect the additional value from the services provided.

A fee-based or fee-only advisor will have access to a wide range of additional services that can add significant value. The fee they charge should reflect the level of services they provide and value you receive from these services.

The Bottom Line?

1. When evaluating investment advisors, selecting the advisor with the lowest fee may not always be the most prudent decision.
2. To get full value for the fees you are paying, you should hire a wealth advisor or financial planner who offers, or has access to, fully integrated investment and wealth management services.
3. Wealth advisors who offer, or have access to, an investment management team will have a disciplined asset allocation process designed specifically for your unique needs.
4. Some wealth advisors offer or have access to private money managers that focus on maximizing your after-tax rate of return. Taxes are probably one of the largest expenditures that you will make over your lifetime.

Check your investment management fees. If you are already paying the standard embedded mutual fund management fee between 2% – 2.75% and are only getting investment advice, you should ask your advisor if they can offer integrated wealth management services.

READY TO SELL YOUR BUSINESS?

Integrated Wealth Management

Helping Your Family	Enjoying Your Lifestyle	Anticipating the Future	Creating Financial Comfort	Leaving a Legacy
Helping Children — Education; Gifting strategies; Business funding	**Home** — Investing proceeds; utilizing equity; Vacation home funding; Home insurance	**Health Changes** — Disability; Critical illness; Life insurance; Long-term care	**Managing Nest Egg** — Asset allocation; Investment selection; Tax planning; Income options	**Wills & Instructions** — Estate plan; Tax planning; Trust services; Asset management
Helping Parents — Long-term care; Managing estate; Care giving	**Leisure & Travel** — Remote banking access; Travel insurance; Emergency fund; Foreign tax rules	**New Opportunities** — Investment funding; Short-term financing; Loans; Emergency funds	**Income planning** — Tax planning; Income layering; RRSP conversion; Minimization strategies	**Charitable Giving** — Planned giving strategy; Tax planning; Estate bequest
Unexpected Demands — Emergency fund; Disability; Critical illness; Life insurance	**Work Options** — Tax planning; Benefit plan; Income management	**Business Succession** — Business valuation; Tax planning; Investing proceeds; Financial purchase	**Minimizing Taxes** — Tax planning; Asset selection; Income layering; Tax-loss selling	**Living Legacy** — Gifting family; Gifting community; Charitable giving
Protecting Family — Disability; Critical illness; Life insurance; Long-term ca...	**Protecting Li...** — Disability/Cri...; Life insurance; Cash flow pr...	**Life on your t...** — Wealth mana...; Portfolio reva...; Cash flow an...; Benefits and...	**Savings & Sp...** — Retirement fl...; Systematic w...; Systematic p...	**Maximizing I...** — Universal & v...; Segregated f...; Testamentari...; Family trusts

Source Published with Permission: Barry LaValley, President, The Retirement Lifestyle Center

117

If your advisor is unable to offer these services, you may want to consider the services of a *Wealth Advisor* or financial planner who offers, or has access to integrated wealth management services.

In many cases, your overall cost for investment management and wealth planning advice is available to you for the same fee or even less than what you may already be paying your current financial advisor for just their investment advice alone!

CHAPTER 24

WHAT COMPREHENSIVE SERVICES SHOULD MY ADVISOR BE OFFERING?

What you pay a Wealth Advisor will depend on the level of services offered. The fee could be as low as 1.5% for pure investment advice to as high as 2.5% for integrated investment and wealth management advice.

These services should include:
1. Comprehensive Reporting
2. A Personal Investment Plan
3. True Global Portfolio Diversification
4. Portfolio Diversification by Industry

5. Portfolio Diversification by Investment Style: Growth, Value and Alpha
6. Portfolio Tax Deferral on Non-Registered Accounts
7. Portfolio Downside Risk Management
8. Regular Portfolio Rebalancing
9. Dynamic Currency Hedging
10. A Backing of a Professional Portfolio Management Team
11. A Dedicated Investment Management Team Overseeing the Portfolio Managers
12. Custom Portfolio Design
13. Investment Fee Transparency
14. A Financial Plan
15. A Risk Management Plan
16. A Personal Tax Plan
17. A Business / Farm Tax Plan
18. A Business / Farm Succession Plan
19. An Estate Plan

READY TO SELL YOUR BUSINESS?

Wealth Planning Strategies

- Financial Analysis & Planning
- Investment Planning
- Tax Planning Strategies / Executive Compensation Strategies
- Business Succession / Pre-Sale / Post-Sale Planning
- Asset Protection
- Estate Planning / Trusts / Risk Management
- Charitable Giving / Philanthropy
- Financial Literacy for Children
- Retirement Planning

Source: Assante Wealth Management Personal Wealth Management Presentation.

CHAPTER 25

50 WAYS WEALTH ADVISORS BENEFIT THEIR CLIENTS

Wealth advisors build strong relationships and partnerships with their clients by:

1. Being honest with you, appreciating and valuing you.
2. Caring about you and your money more than anyone who does not share your surname.
3. Being someone whom you can trust and get advice from for all your financial matters.
4. Understanding what money means to you and what motivates you.

5. Listening and asking questions to help you identify and articulate your needs, goals and objectives.
6. Working with you to alleviate worries that keep you awake at night.
7. Coaching you to do the things that will help accomplish your goals.
8. Monitoring changes in your life and family situation.
9. Guiding you through difficult periods in the stock market by sharing a historical perspective.
10. Acting as a sounding/discussion board for ideas you are considering.
11. Providing guidance on what course you should take and giving you an objective perspective.
12. Anticipating future changes and proactively working through them with you.
13. Keeping you on track.

Wealth advisors provide customized wealth planning services by:

14. Helping you make important financial-related decisions.
15. Helping organize and prioritize your financial life.

16. Helping you determine where you are at present.
17. Helping you formalize realistic goals and put them in writing.
18. Making specific recommendations to help you meet your goals.
19. Establishing a clear strategy and action plan.
20. Suggesting creative alternatives that you may not have considered.
21. Preparing an investment policy statement for you.
22. Reviewing and recommending life insurance policies to protect your family.
23. Staying up to date on tax law changes.
24. Helping you reduce your taxes by reviewing your tax returns for possible savings.
25. Working with your tax and legal advisors and other professionals to facilitate and coordinate your overall financial plans.
26. Identifying your saving shortfalls.
27. Helping establish your will and estate, retirement and business succession plans.
28. Helping you transfer wealth efficiently to the next generation.
29. Developing and monitoring a strategy for debt reduction.

Wealth advisors construct personalized client portfolios by:

30. Preparing an asset allocation strategy for you to diversify your investments and achieve the best rate of return for your level of risk tolerance.
31. Performing due diligence on money managers and mutual fund managers to ensure appropriate investment recommendations.
32. Staying up to date with changes in the investment world.
33. Reviewing and revising your portfolio as conditions change.
34. Helping consolidate, simplify and improve your investment performance.
35. Monitoring your investments and converting them into income as needed.
36. Helping you establish better planning and record keeping.
37. Exploring and reviewing potential income-splitting and tax-minimization strategies with you.
38. Recommending and completing appropriate tax-loss selling solutions.
39. Repositioning investments to take full advantage of tax rules.

Wealth advisors ensure they offer exceptional service by:

40. Providing full disclosure and transparency on their fees and processes.
41. Proactively keeping in touch with you by providing customized and personalized information.
42. Providing referrals to and liaising with other professionals such as accountants, actuaries, tax lawyers, as needed.
43. Being only a telephone call away to answer financial questions for you.
44. Serving as a human glossary of financial terms such as beta, P/E ratio, and Sharpe ratio.
45. Listening and providing feedback in a way that a magazine or newsletter writer cannot.
46. Helping educate your children and grandchildren about investments and financial concepts.
47. Educating you on retirement, savings and other financial topics.
48. Helping with other non-financial advice.
49. Providing easy-to-read account statements and reports.
50. Holding seminars to educate you on significant and/or new financial concepts.

CHAPTER 26

CONCLUSION

Conclusion

As you can see if you have gone through this information in detail, managing your financial assets is much more than handing off the decision-making to a financial advisor (stockbroker, mutual fund salesman, insurance salesman or the nice lady at the bank).

It involves understanding all types of financial advisors and which services they offer.

It also means understanding how they are paid for their services (no one works for free).

It also means that you get what you pay for.

Better services will cost more initially, but good advice will save you money, taxes and headaches.

The wealth you accumulate over the years will be professionally managed and provide for your family and charitable interests.

Take the Next Step

Your Family Business Transition Strategy™ is an exclusive service available to clients of Assante Private Client Managed Portfolios.

If you're like most business owners, you have built up a sizable nest egg.

However, the journey building that nest-egg may have been somewhat haphazard.

You may have multiple investment accounts with multiple advisors.

You have a rough idea of how much you have saved, but it's a challenge collecting all those investment statements to get a clear picture of what you have.

And when you have everything together you still do not have a good handle on how well all your investments are doing, whether you are on track to meeting your retirement goals, or how much you are paying in fees for investment advice.

CHAPTER 27

YOUR OPTIMAL PORTFOLIO SOLUTION

Retire with confidence

Your Optimal Portfolio Solution™ ...

...is a customized portfolio solution designed around your unique needs. It is designed to maximize your investment growth tax efficiently while staying within your comfort zone in up markets as well as protecting your capital in down markets.

No single investment is right for every point in time. A properly constructed portfolio is needed to help smooth out the markets' ups and downs.

Portfolio diversification is the key. By combining different styles of investments, different asset classes and exposure to various geographic regions, your portfolio is positioned to grow to its potential.

The tax effectiveness of your investments is addressed through tax optimization in your investment portfolio and the use of tax-advantaged investment structures. As you know – it's not how much you make that counts, it's what you get to keep that matters!

READY TO SELL YOUR BUSINESS?

8 Steps to Creating a Portfolio That Is Right For YOU! ...

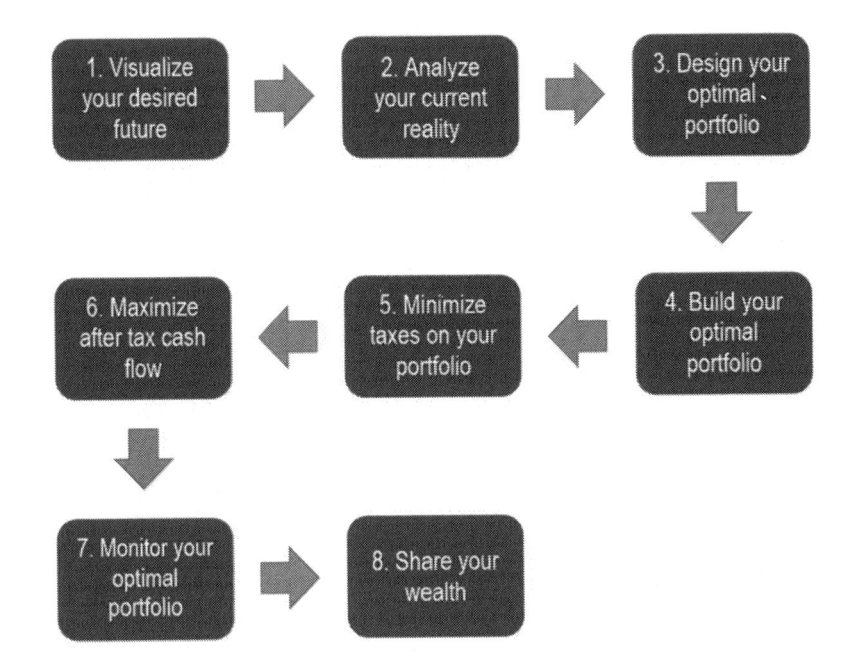

1. Visualize your desired future →
2. Analyze your current reality →
3. Design your optimal portfolio ↓
4. Build your optimal portfolio ←
5. Minimize taxes on your portfolio ←
6. Maximize after tax cash flow ↓
7. Monitor your optimal portfolio →
8. Share your wealth

Step 1 - VISUALIZE – your desired future

Your Money Conversation™

1. Visualize your desired future

Our relationship with you begins with us having a conversation with you about your money.

We take the time to really get to know your intimate fears challenges, advantages, excitements, opportunities, lifetime goals and aspirations for you, your family and legacy.

We spend considerable amount of time helping you visualize your need for income, time horizon, risk tolerance, liquidity requirements, growth expectations, income tax characteristics, anticipated changes in your lifestyle and economic variables such as inflation and market volatility.

Result: Vision | Investment: Complimentary

Step 2 - ANALYZE – your current reality

Your Current Reality Audit™

2. Analyze your current reality

Next, we need to know if you are on track to achieving your retirement goals, so before we can begin the process of creating **Your Optimal Portfolio™**, we need to understand your current reality.

This involves exploring all the areas of your personal and family life that have a financial impact on your wealth.

This results in a high-level projection of your net wealth and sufficiency of financial resources needed to help you meet the objectives revealed in **Your Money Conversation™**.

Result: Understanding | Investment: Complimentary

Step 3 - DESIGN – your optimal portfolio

Your Optimal Portfolio Blueprint™

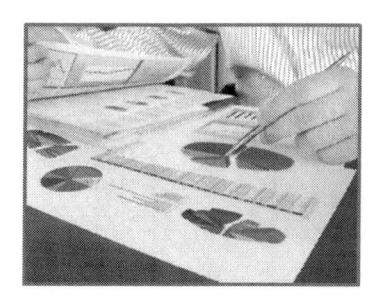

3. Design your optimal portfolio

Before we can build **Your Optimal Portfolio™** you need a blueprint of how your money will be managed.

We begin by creating a document called an Investment Policy Statement (**IPS**). This document captures what we learned about you in **Your Money Conversation™** and **Your Current Reality Audit™**.

The IPS summarizes your needs for:
- Income
- Time horizon
- Risk tolerance
- Liquidity requirements
- Growth expectations

- Income tax characteristics
- Anticipated changes in lifestyle
- Economic variables such as inflation and market volatility

The IPS outlines the strategies the investment management team will employ to build **Your Optimal Portfolio**™. This provides a blueprint of how the team at Assante Private Client, a division of CI Private Counsel LP will manage your investments.

Result:

Personalized Investment Plan | Investment: Complimentary

Step 4 - BUILD – your optimal portfolio

Your Optimal Portfolio™

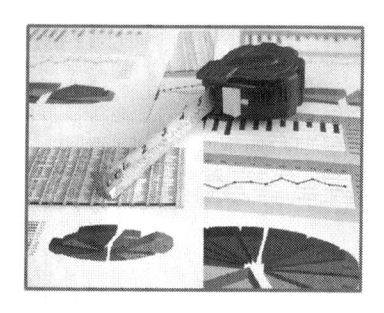

4. Build your optimal portfolio

The next step is to hire the investment management team of Assante Private Client, a division of CI Private Counsel LP to build **Your Optimal Portfolio™** as outlined in **Your Optimal Portfolio Blueprint™**.

Your Optimal Portfolio™ is designed to maximize your investment growth while staying within your comfort zone in up markets as well as protect your capital in down markets.

This is achieved by combining different investment styles, asset classes and exposure to various geographic regions and automatic rebalancing.

Tax efficiency is achieved by the use of tax-advantaged investment structures and appropriate tax planning strategies to minimize overall family tax liability on your investments.

Result:

Your Optimal Portfolio™ | Investment: $250,000

Step 5 - MINIMIZE – taxes on your optimal portfolio

Your Tax Advantaged Solution™

5. Minimize taxes on your portfolio

The more you have the more you pay: it's a fact of life, or is it? Tax planning is an important component of **Your Optimal Portfolio Solution™**, since taxes can have a significant impact on your wealth and eventual legacy.

For your investments held outside of a registered plan, company investment account or trusts, tax efficiency is a critical issue. Since your non-registered assets are not sheltered from taxes, rebalancing transactions and distributions are taxed, adding up to a heavy tax burden.

The tax effectiveness of your investments is addressed through tax optimization of **Your Optimal Portfolio™** and the use of tax-advantaged investment structures to reduce or defer highly taxed interest income and earn tax-efficient dividends or capital gains.

By combining the tax expertise of our wealth planning group and the investment management team, we can create opportunities for deferring, minimizing or eliminating taxes. As you know – it's not how much you make that counts, it's what you get to keep that matters!

Result: More Money| Investment: Complimentary

Step 6 - MAXIMIZE – your after-tax cash flow

Your Tax Efficient Cash Flow Solution™

6. Maximize after tax cash flow

For Retiring Business Owners, **Your Tax Efficient Cash Flow Solution™** will allow you to extend the life of **Your Optimal Portfolio™** by allowing you to draw monthly cash flow tax-efficiently, while maintaining potential for growth.

Your Tax Efficient Cash Flow Solution™ returns your original principle first without attracting taxable income in the early years of withdrawal, while deferring the growth in the form of unrealized capital gains.

Since you are not paying taxes on the money returned to you on your original principle, your annual withdrawal is reduced by the amount of taxes you would have otherwise paid.

This extends the life of **Your Optimal Portfolio™** by allowing the tax saved to stay in **Your Optimal Portfolio™** and continue to grow until your original principle has been returned to you.

Once your original principle has been returned to you, you are left with unrealized capital gains in **Your Optimal Portfolio™**. The remaining unrealized gains are returned to you next and are taxed at the capital gains rate which is taxed at ½ your marginal tax rate. Receiving income in the form of capital gains is more efficient than interest income from bank deposits or bonds.

This further extends the life of **Your Optimal Portfolio™** as you only need to withdraw 50% of the tax amount in addition to your monthly income needs.

Result:

Your money lasts longer | Investment: Tailored to your needs

Step 7 - MONITOR – your optimal portfolio

Your Optimal Portfolio Monitor™

7. Monitor your optimal portfolio

Once **Your Optimal Portfolio™** has been implemented, our work is not done.

We meet with you every six to twelve months and more often if necessary to monitor your portfolio and to document any major changes in your personal or financial situation that may require us to make adjustments to **Your Optimal Portfolio™**.

We will also begin work on **Your Family Wealth Foundation™** to help you achieve your lifetime aspirations and ensure you leave a legacy of significance for your family and cherished causes.

Result: Keeping your portfolio optimized | Investment: Tailored to your needs

Step 8 - OPTIMIZE – your wealth

Your Family Wealth Foundation™

8. Share your wealth

Your Family Wealth Foundation™ is where we empower you to simplify your life and optimize your wealth so you can achieve your family's multi-generational goals of wealth accumulation, preservation and distribution.

We work extensively with the Wealth Planning Group of Assante Private Client, a division of CI Private Counsel LP., a team of tax, legal and estate specialists along with your own legal and accounting professionals to consolidate your sophisticated complex financial reality.

We analyze a variety of possible solutions including wealth preservation and tax planning strategies across multiple generations to protect and enhance your wealth.

We explore strategies and solutions that may help you to achieve your family's desired future. The outcome—a legacy of significance for your family and cherished causes.

Result: Your Family Wealth Foundation | Investment: Complimentary

CHAPTER 28

THE SECOND OPINION PORTFOLIO AUDIT™

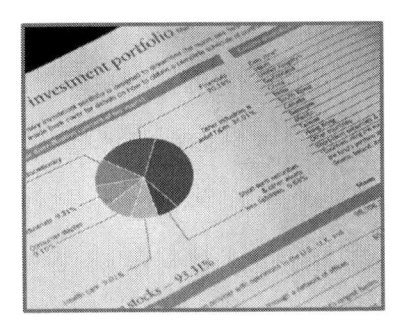

You may be asking yourself the following questions:

1. Have I saved enough?
2. What is the combined average annual return on all my investments this past year, over the past three, five or ten years?
3. Will these returns help me achieve my goals short term AND long term?
4. Am I comfortable with the risk level of my investments?

5. Can I reduce the tax payable on my investment income?
6. How much am I paying in fees and how are those fees affecting my investment returns?
7. What value am I really getting for the fees I am paying?

Fortunately, I have good news to announce!

"I am offering a **COMPLIMENTARY** Second Opinion Portfolio Audit and Investment Strategy for Families with $250,000 or More in Investable Assets Who Want to Know if Their Investments Are Good Enough to Help Them Reach Their Retirement Goals"

The Second-Opinion Portfolio Audit™ is a technical-sounding name for a simple idea: a detailed analysis of your current portfolio, summarizing all your investments itemizing; the fees, what you are getting for those fees, how well your investments are doing and if your portfolio is structured to minimize taxes and risk.

I will listen to you to discover your personal financial situation, goals, comfort level, risk tolerance and needs. This will help me have a Personalized Investment Strategy* created for you which will allow me to better assess whether your current portfolio is good enough to help you reach your retirement goals. This investment strategy* will outline how your investments should be managed based on your personal situation and is how the investment management team we recommend to our clients would manage your money should you decide to become a client.

Should you decide to accept the recommendations outlined in the Personalized Investment Strategy* and become a client you will also receive a comprehensive Financial Plan and Estate Plan at no additional charge if you have a minimum of $250,000 invested in Evolution Private Managed Accounts and a comprehensive Wealth Plan if you have a minimum of $1,000,000 invested in Private Client Managed Portfolios.

In many cases, your overall cost for investment management and wealth planning advice is available to you for the same fee or even less than what you may already be paying your current financial advisor for just their investment advice alone!

So, What's My Motivation?

My goal is really very straight forward:

- To help you grow your money so that you can achieve financial freedom, security and peace of mind and help you avoid the mistakes my father made.
- To provide you with actionable strategies that you can use to grow your wealth.
- To protect your wealth and help you create a legacy for your family for generations to come.

I am aligned with a team of financial experts that can help me put you on **Your Personal Path to Financial Freedom, Security & Peace of Mind™**.

I am confident that by providing you with a complimentary Personalized Investment Strategy* you will want to become a client.

I believe that it is far easier to show you a sample of what you can expect as a client, rather than make a promise that you can only experience if you become a client.

Some financial advisors make promises but sadly, cannot or do not deliver on those promises.

By showing you what it is like to be one of my clients, I am very confident you will make the decision to become a client.

If after reviewing your **Personalized Investment Strategy**, you decide that you are not ready to become a client, or you do not see the value in what I have provided, or you are extremely happy with your current financial advisor, you are free to keep everything I have provided you, to use with your current financial advisor without charge.

You are welcome to call me anytime during regular business hours. If I am unavailable and you have left a message, I guarantee that I will return your call within 24 hours.

You see, I believe that by providing exceptional value even before you become a client, you will want to become a client.

Are you the right Client?

Often, potential clients like you wonder if our recommended programs are suitable for them.

Here are some ways to know if we can assist you in your wealth creation and preservation.

Are you someone who:

1. is an individual in the 50+ age group with minimum investible assets of $250,000 or more?
2. is looking forward to retirement or has recently retired?
3. has worked hard to reach a secure place where they're able to take care of their family and contribute to their community?
4. would rather spend their time with their family doing the things that are important to their family?
5. realizes that retirement planning is much more than portfolio performance or just about numbers?
6. is ready to establish a long-term plan that will assure them of their family's future security?
7. Doesn't have the desire, expertise, or the extra time to manage their retirement investment portfolio?
8. has decided to consider delegating their financial matters to a skilled, experienced and dependable group of financial planning and investment professionals?
9. is looking for a proactive and personalized service?

READY TO SELL YOUR BUSINESS?

I look forward to meeting you to complete...

YOUR Second Opinion Portfolio Audit™
You can contact me Adrian Spitters at:
604.855.6846 – aspitters@assante.com
Or visit
www.secondopinionportfolioaudit.com

Go ahead, call for a personal consultation.
No obligation whatsoever
I want you to be an informed consumer – one who can stare down those imminent threats, and sleep peacefully.

DOWNLOAD MY FREE BOOK

Do you have the right financial advisor working for you? Not sure?
Find out in my new book:
Who's Investing Your Money?
Learn How to Ask the Right Questions to Select the Best Financial Advisor for Your Situation
To get your free book visit:
www.whosinvestingyourmoney.com

APPENDIX

Adrian Spitters •

Senior Wealth Advisor •

Assante Capital Management Ltd.

604 - 855 - 6846 •

aspitters@assante.com

Web: www.yourbusinesstransitionadvisor.ca

Published by

HeartBeat Productions Inc.

Box 633

Abbotsford, BC

Canada V2T 6Z8

email: **info@heartbeat1.com**

604.852.3761

CHAPTER 29

APPENDIX

TAX PLANNING FOR THE SALE OF YOUR BUSINESS

This Guide is Provided Courtesy of Assante Wealth Management.

The following Reference Guide is one in a series of Reference Guides available through the Wealth Planning Group of Assante Private Client, a division of CI Private Counsel LP, and is reproduced with permission. Assante Private Client provides Integrated Wealth Management Solutions to Assante Wealth Management's high net worth clients across Canada. My association with Assante Wealth Management gives me access to this group, which is comprised of lawyers, accountants, financial analysts, insurance experts, business succession planning, farm succession planning and estate planning professionals.

Reference Guide

Tax Planning for The Sale of Your Business

If you own a corporation that carries on an active business, you may be in a position at some point to consider the sale of your business.

This reference guide sets out some of the important tax issues that you should consider.

SHARE SALE vs ASSET SALE

The sale of an incorporated business can be accomplished either through the sale of the corporation's assets or the sale of shares of the corporation. The asset sale versus share sale decision requires consideration of many tax and non-tax issues. However, tax will generally play a significant role in the decision.

As a general rule, the vendor of an incorporated business would prefer to sell shares, while the purchaser would prefer to buy assets. For the vendor, the tax cost will generally be less in the case of a share sale. For the purchaser, an asset purchase will result in a greater cost base for the underlying assets of the business, and therefore a greater cost base on which to claim depreciation. In addition, with an asset purchase, the purchaser can recognize and depreciate for tax purposes any goodwill associated with the business.

A non-tax reason that a purchaser would rather purchase assets is the potential liabilities that may exist in the corporation, which would remain if the purchaser acquired the shares of the corporation. By buying the assets of an existing corporation instead, and carrying on the business in a new corporation, the purchaser will only inherit those liabilities that it specifically assumes. This would be of particular concern if the nature of the business were such that it could give rise to significant potential unrecorded liabilities (e.g. liability with respect to environmental damage.) However, it should be noted that an asset sale may be subject to sales tax, GST or HST and land transfer tax, which would be payable by the purchaser. In addition, an asset purchase can be a more complex transaction to implement, because each asset must be transferred and registered in the name of the purchaser.

In either case, whether on a sale of shares or assets, there are opportunities for the vendor to minimize tax.

MINIMIZING TAX ON A SHARE SALE

There are several methods to reduce or defer the tax that the vendor will pay on a sale of shares.

CAPITAL GAINS EXEMPTION

Many sale transactions are structured around the vendor's ability to claim the capital gains exemption in respect of the disposition of shares of a qualified small business corporation (QSBC shares). The exemption limit was set at $800,000 in 2014 and is indexed for inflation in subsequent years.

The enhanced capital gains exemption is available only to individuals who are resident in Canada throughout the year. It is reduced to the extent that capital gains exemptions were claimed in previous taxation years[6]. The amount of the exemption that may be claimed may also be reduced by any net capital losses claimed by the individual for the year, any allowable business investment losses claimed by the individual and the individual's cumulative net investment loss at the end of the year.

---

[6] The enhanced capital gains exemption available upon the disposition of QSBC shares may be reduced to the extent that the individual has previously used the general exemption of $100,000, which was repealed in 1994, or any capital gains exemption previously claimed related to QSBC shares or certain qualified farm or fishing property.

In addition, care should be taken if capital losses (such as on personal non-registered investment assets) are realized in the same year that a capital gain eligible for the capital gains exemption is realized. As the allowable capital losses, must first be offset against eligible capital gains realized in the year, this can result in situations where the gain is shielded by the current losses rather than the capital gains exemption.

Additionally, certain rules provide that the exemption may be denied where it can reasonably be concluded that a significant part of an individual's capital gain results from the fact that the shares (other than certain prescribed shares) have paid low or no dividends or that dividends paid were less than 90% of the annual rate of return that a prudent investor would expect to receive. These rules prevent the conversion of dividends into exempt capital gains through the use of shares with attributes designed specifically to yield capital gains by not paying dividends where dividends could reasonably be expected.

QSBC SHARE

In order to qualify for the enhanced capital gains exemption, an individual must dispose of a share of a qualified small business corporation or QSBC. A QSBC share of an individual is defined to be a share of the capital stock of a corporation that meets the following criteria:

- **Determination Time Asset Test:** At any time (the Determination Time) it is a share of a small business corporation owned by the individual. In order to qualify as a small business corporation, it is required that the corporation be a Canadian-controlled private corporation (CCPC), all or substantially all of the fair market value of the assets of which were used in an active business carried on primarily in Canada by the corporation or a related corporation, or certain shares and indebtedness of a connected small business corporation, or any combination of such assets. The Canada Revenue Agency (CRA) has generally interpreted the phrase "all or substantially all" to mean 90%.

- **24 Month Ownership Test:** In the 24 months preceding the Determination Time, the share was not owned by anyone not related to the individual.

- **24-Month Asset Test:**
  * Where the situation involves only one corporation (i.e. not a situation in which a holding company owns an operating company), in the 24 months preceding the Determination Time, the share was a share of a CCPC, more than 50% of the fair market value of the assets of which must have been attributable to assets used principally in an active business carried on primarily in Canada by the corporation or a related corporation, or certain shares or indebtedness of a connected corporation, or any combination of such assets.
  * Where the share being considered is a share of a holding corporation (i.e., where there is a tiered structure, with the individual directly owning shares in a holding company, which in turn holds shares in the operating company), additional considerations apply, and the 24-month business asset test may be more stringent. If 90% or more of the holding company's assets are either active assets and/or investments in connected CCPCs, then the connected company or companies need only meet the 50% test. However, if the holding company does not meet this 90% test, then the connected company or companies must meet the 90% test throughout the 24-month period and the

holding company must meet the 50% test. Essentially, it will be necessary for either the holding corporation or its connected subsidiary or subsidiaries to meet the 90% threshold throughout the 24-month period preceding the disposition of the shares.

NON-ELIGIBLE ASSETS - PURIFICATION OF A CORPORATION

Given the above asset tests, ownership by a corporation of non-eligible assets such as significant reserves of cash or investment assets may therefore disqualify the shares of a corporation as QSBC shares. This would occur if those non-eligible assets exceed 10% of the fair market value of all assets of the corporation at the time of disposition, or 50% of the fair market value of all assets of the corporation during the 24 months preceding the time of disposition (assuming the subsidiary company meets the 90% test throughout the 24-month period).

The determination as to whether assets are eligible active business assets or non-eligible assets for the purposes of the tests described above must be made in light of all the facts and requirements of the specific business, in consultation with professional advisors. In a seasonal business, for example, the proportion of cash or investment assets required in the business activities may be higher than in a non-seasonal business.

If a corporation does not meet the 24-month asset test, there are various strategies available to purify the corporation for the purposes of the enhanced capital gains exemption by removing excess non-eligible assets. However, it can take two years or more for the shares to meet the QSBC definition after purification. It is therefore important to begin reviewing the status of your corporation's shares sooner rather than later. This would be an efficient strategy prior to the sale of a business. It would also be important to examine this issue as part of the planning of an estate freeze. A careful review of certain tax rules that target "surplus stripping" is necessary whenever planning involving inter-corporate dividends is being considered.

USE OF MULTIPLE EXEMPTIONS

An additional planning technique available to a vendor of shares is to introduce children and other family members as shareholders of the corporation, typically through the use of a family trust and a corporate reorganization. If the shares of the corporation rise in value and are later sold, the family members will incur a capital gain proportionate to the value of the shares they hold, and may potentially shield the gain by using their own lifetime capital gains exemption.

Since the newly introduced shareholders will only incur gains (and thereby utilize the capital gains exemption) to the extent that the fair market value of their shares increases after they became shareholders, utilization of this technique requires planning well in advance of a contemplated share sale.

SHARE SALE TO A NON-ARM'S LENGTH CORPORATION

Note that special rules can apply when an individual sells shares to a corporation with which the individual does not deal at arm's length under the income tax legislation. If applicable, the rules will deem a vendor to receive proceeds in the form of deemed dividends instead of capital gains, which would prevent the vendor from being able to claim the enhanced capital gains exemption to shield gains from taxation. Careful planning considerations are therefore involved in any situation where an individual proposes to sell shares to a non-arm's length corporation.

PAYMENTS FROM AVAILABLE TAX POOLS

Another method of minimizing tax is to remove value from the corporation prior to the sale where the tax cost of the removal is less than the tax cost of the capital gain that would otherwise arise. The following are some examples of how this might be accomplished:

SHAREHOLDER LOANS

Amounts owing by a corporation to its shareholders can be repaid without tax. These amounts should be repaid prior to a sale. This payment should have no effect on the purchase price, as it would result in a decrease in both the assets (i.e. cash) and the liabilities of the corporation in an equivalent amount.

CAPITAL DIVIDEND ACCOUNT

The balance in the corporation's capital dividend account (CDA) may be distributed to its shareholders without triggering personal tax. A CDA primarily arises from three possible sources: the tax-free portion of any capital gains realized by the corporation (reduced by capital losses), life insurance proceeds received by the corporation, and capital dividends received by the corporation.

A vendor should extract the balance of the CDA account by paying out capital dividends prior to selling shares of the corporation. This would reduce the value of the corporation, which would in turn reduce the purchase price subject to tax.

SAFE INCOME

Safe Income represents the earnings of a corporation that can be extracted and passed on to another corporate entity (by way of an inter-corporate dividend) without incurring tax at the corporate level. Tax on these earnings is deferred until they are extracted from that corporation and paid to the individual shareholders. A vendor would consider paying a safe income dividend if the vendor intends to leave funds in a remaining corporation to achieve a tax deferral.

It should be noted that to pay a safe income dividend, costs would be incurred in the calculation of safe income as well as a corporate reorganization (if necessary). An estimate of those costs should be obtained from your professional advisors, in order to assess whether the benefits of this strategy outweigh the potential costs.

RETIRING ALLOWANCE

Another strategy used to defer tax (and, if the deferral is long enough, to save tax) is to have the corporation pay to the vendor(s) a retiring allowance prior to the sale. The payment of a retiring allowance would decrease the value of the corporation and would therefore decrease the purchase price that would be subject to tax.

If the vendor was employed by the corporation prior to 1996, a portion of the retiring allowance received by the vendor may be transferred to an RRSP, and would then not be subject to tax until withdrawn from the RRSP. That portion is calculated as follows:

- $2,000 for every year of employment prior to 1996, plus
- $1,500 for every year of employment prior to 1989 with respect to which employer contributions to a registered pension plan or deferred profit sharing plan had not vested.

In order for the payment to constitute a retiring allowance, the vendor(s) would have to actually cease employment with the corporation and could not remain on as consultants. However, the vendor could still remain as a director, provided the compensation is nominal.

CAPITAL GAIN ROLLOVER

Under the income tax legislation, an individual can defer all or a portion of a capital gain when the individual disposes of shares of an eligible small business corporation and uses the proceeds to invest in new shares of another eligible small business corporation (sometimes referred to as replacement shares). This deferral is effected by the cost base of the replacement shares being reduced by the amount of the capital gain deferred.

An investment in an eligible small business corporation, whether being sold or acquired, must generally have the following characteristics:

- the investment must be, or must have been, in the form of common shares issued from treasury (that is, acquired directly from the corporation, not purchased from a shareholder)
- at the time the shares are issued and throughout the period that they are held, the corporation is a CCPC with 90% or more of its assets either:
  * used principally in carrying on an active business in Canada, or
  * being shares of a related eligible small business
- before and after the time the investment is made, the total carrying value of its assets and those of related corporations does not exceed $50,000,000. (The carrying value refers to the value arrived at in accordance with generally accepted accounting principles used in Canada.)

In order for the gain to be deferred, the shares must be owned by the individual throughout the 185-day period immediately prior to the disposition. In addition, the purchase of replacement shares must be made either in the year of disposition of the previous investment, or within 120 days after the end of that year. The replacement shares must also be designated as such in the individual's tax return.

The maximum capital gain that can be deferred is based on the proportion of the proceeds received from the disposition that are reinvested in eligible investments.

If you have plans to reinvest any of the proceeds from the sale of a business in another business venture, you should discuss this potential deferral with your professional advisors.

DEFER PAYMENT OF THE PURCHASE PRICE

Deferring the payment and receipt of the purchase price is another way to defer tax. Note, however, that to the extent that a vendor agrees to defer the receipt of the purchase price, the vendor is financing the acquisition. In such cases, the vendor should ensure that any unpaid amounts are properly secured.

CAPITAL GAINS RESERVE

As a general rule, tax is payable when the business is sold, regardless of when the purchase price is paid. However, in certain circumstances, a reserve may be available to the vendor. The effect of the reserve is to spread out the capital gain over more than one taxation year.

In a typical situation, the vendor and purchaser will fix the purchase price and agree that it will be payable in annual installments. If the sale agreement is properly structured, the proceeds generally will not be taxable until they are actually received (subject to a maximum deferral of five years in most situations, or ten years in certain cases involving dispositions of qualifying private corporation shares, family farm or fishing property by a parent to a child).

ROLLOVER FOR SHARES

Subsection 85(1) of the Income Tax Act provides for a rollover when the vendor receives consideration that includes shares of the purchaser (where the purchaser is a corporation). This is, in effect, a deferral of payment, since the vendor would receive no cash until the shares are sold or redeemed. If the vendor receives freely tradable shares of the purchaser corporation, the tax liability would be realized when the vendor sells the shares on the open market (if they are shares of a public company) or as the shares are redeemed by the purchaser corporation.

MINIMIZING TAX ON AN ASSET SALE

There are a few methods to reduce the tax that the vendor (in this case, the corporation) will pay on an asset sale.

ALLOCATION OF PURCHASE PRICE

When an asset sale is contemplated, the allocation of the purchase price will be a key issue. For the purchaser, it will be important to maximize the tax cost basis for the assets it is purchasing, so that it can obtain the most beneficial write-off of this basis over time. The purchaser may therefore place greater emphasis on obtaining cost base for depreciable property (such as buildings or equipment) rather than non-depreciable items (such as land). However, the most beneficial position for the vendor from a tax perspective may differ significantly depending on the nature of the assets being sold.

Any allocation, however, cannot be driven solely by

the tax considerations of either party. It is important that any allocation consider the regulations applicable to this issue under the Income Tax Act. Since this is a complex area, professional advisors should be consulted in determining the most appropriate allocation based on your circumstances.

DEFER PAYMENT OF THE PURCHASE PRICE

The methods discussed above for deferring the payment of the purchase price on a share sale will also apply to the corporate vendor on an asset sale.

Conclusion

As outlined in this reference guide, there are several tax planning opportunities when you are considering a sale of your business. There may be additional strategies beyond those discussed here, depending on the particular circumstances of the vendor and the purchaser. In all cases, professional legal and accounting advice, as well as proper planning and documentation, are essential.

Adrian Spitters
FCSI, CFP, FMA
Senior Wealth Advisor

I grew up on a dairy farm on Nicomen Island near Mission, BC and have immediate family and relatives operating dairy, poultry and crop farms. As co-executor (with two brothers) of my father's estate, I know all too well the result of not having a proper farm transition plan in place.

Our dad had a poorly executed, unworkable Will and a non-existent farm succession plan. This led to family discord. Despite receiving the majority of the assets, the brother who inherited the farm suffered financial distress and became insolvent. A proper transition plan would have helped him get the financial and farm management training he needed.

Today, I work as a Senior Wealth Advisor with Assante Capital Management Ltd., with extensive experience in integrated family wealth planning. I provide wealth advisory services to multi-generational families, family businesses and farm families. This includes helping them grow, protect and preserve their family assets, wealth and legacy.

In my 29 years in the business, this is what I've seen: that all Canadians, especially business owners, need and want personalized financial advice that helps them achieve their life goals.

It is very clear to me that whether you have a transition plan in place or not, one day you will transfer your business to your children, extended family or sell to a third party. The question is, will it be on your terms **(voluntarily)**, or someone else's **(involuntarily)**?

Adrian Spitters •
Senior Wealth Advisor •
Assante Capital Management Ltd.
604 - 855 - 6846 •
<u>aspitters@assante.com</u>

READY TO SELL YOUR BUSINESS?

The opinions expressed are those of the author and not necessarily those of Assante Capital Management Ltd.

Evolution Private Managed Account services are managed by CI Investments Inc. ("CI"). Commissions, trailing commissions, management fees, and expenses may all be associated with mutual fund investments in Evolution Private Managed Accounts and the use of Asset Management Service. Mutual funds are not guaranteed, their values change frequently and past performance may not be repeated. Please read the prospectus and consult your Assante Advisor before investing. Evolution is a registered trademark of CI Investments Inc. Assante is an indirect, wholly-owned subsidiary of CI Financial Corp. ("CI"). The principal business of CI is the management, marketing, distribution and administration of mutual funds, segregated funds and other fee-earning investment products for Canadian investors through its wholly-owned subsidiary CI Investments Inc. If you invest in CI products, CI will, through its ownership of subsidiaries, earn ongoing asset management fees in accordance with applicable prospectus or other offering documents. *Complementary Investment Strategy document refers to an Investment Policy Statement for investments in Evolution Managed Accounts, managed by CI Investments Inc. **This would include a combination of RRSP, TFSA, individual and joint Investment accounts and business investment accounts. ***Financial plans and estate plans for asset levels of $250,000.00 when invested in the Evolution Private Managed Account.

Private Client Managed Portfolios are made available through Assante Private Client, a division of CI Private Counsel LP ("Assante Private Client"). The pools used in the Private Client Managed Portfolios are managed by CI Investments Inc., an affiliate of CI Private Counsel LP. Commissions, trailing commissions, management fees and expenses may all be associated with investments in Private Client Managed Portfolios and the use of other services. The pools used in the Private Client Managed Portfolios are not guaranteed, their values change frequently and past performance may not be repeated. Please consult your advisor before investing. Assante Private Client is a registered adviser under applicable securities legislation. This document is intended solely for information purposes. It is not a sales prospectus, nor should it be construed as an offer or an invitation to take part in an offer. Private Client Managed Portfolios are available exclusively through Assante Capital Management Ltd. – Member of the Canadian Investor Protection Fund and the Investment Industry Regulatory Organization of Canada – and Assante Financial Management Ltd. ®CI Investments, the CI Investments design and Cambridge are registered trademarks of CI Investments Inc. Assante Private Client and the Assante Private Client design are registered trademarks of CI Investments Inc.

This material is provided for general information and is subject to change without notice. Every effort has been made to compile this material from reliable sources however no warranty can be made as to its accuracy or completeness. Before acting on any of the above, please make sure to see me for individual financial advice based on your personal circumstances. Please visit www.assante.com/legal.jsp or contact Assante at 1-800-268-3200 for information with respect to important legal and regulatory disclosures relating to this notice.

Insurance products and services are provided through Performance Financial Consultants Ltd. Tracking # 58293D

Made in the USA
Lexington, KY
31 May 2017